90 Days to Success Marketing and Advertising Your Small Business

Course Technology PTR

A part of Cengage Learning

COURSE TECHNOLOGY
CENGAGE Learning™

Australia, Brazil, Japan, Korea, Mexico, Singapore, Spain, United Kingdom, United States

COURSE TECHNOLOGY
CENGAGE Learning™

90 Days to Success Marketing and Advertising Your Small Business

Mark Hoxie

Publisher and General Manager, Course Technology PTR:
Stacy L. Hiquet

Associate Director of Marketing: Sarah Panella

Manager of Editorial Services:
Heather Talbot

Marketing Manager:
Mark Hughes

Acquisitions Editor:
Mitzi Koontz

Project Editor/Copy Editor:
Cathleen D. Small

Interior Layout Tech:
Judy Littlefield

Cover Designer:
Mike Tanamachi

Indexer: Kelly Talbot
Editing Services

Proofreader: Kelly Talbot
Editing Services

For product information and technology assistance, contact us at **Cengage Learning Customer & Sales Support, 1-800-354-9706**

For permission to use material from this text or product, submit all requests online at **cengage.com/permissions**
Further permissions questions can be e-mailed to **permissionrequest@cengage.com**.

Library of Congress Control Number: 2010936616

ISBN-13: 978-1-4354-5828-4

ISBN-10: 1-4354-5828-1

Course Technology, a part of Cengage Learning
20 Channel Center Street
Boston, MA 02210
USA

Cengage Learning is a leading provider of customized learning solutions with office locations around the globe, including Singapore, the United Kingdom, Australia, Mexico, Brazil, and Japan. Locate your local office at: **international.cengage.com/region**.

Cengage Learning products are represented in Canada by Nelson Education, Ltd.

For your lifelong learning solutions, visit **courseptr.com**.

Visit our corporate Web site at **cengage.com**.

Printed in the United States of America
1 2 3 4 5 6 7 12 11 10

In loving memory of Raymond Hoxie
July 21, 1922–September 15, 2010

Acknowledgments

First and foremost, I would like to thank my acquisitions editor, Mitzi Koontz, at Cengage Learning. You believed in me and this project before even I fully did. To Cathleen Small, my project editor: I must have won the editor lottery when I was awarded the chance to work with you. Your patience, humor, and abilities carried me through this project. Special thanks to Dave Glidden and Russ Holly, who took a chance on an under-qualified candidate and introduced him to the world of advertising almost 10 years ago.

Thank you to my brother, Brendan Hoxie. You taught me not to just think outside the box, but to live outside of it—so far outside that you can't even see it anymore. Scott and Abbey Hoxie, you always make me proud with your accomplishments, and you are always the first to make me feel proud of my own. Michele Nastri, your support and inspiration kept me going through this project. Without you, I would not have had the confidence to follow my dreams—you've encouraged them into my reality. Dan Thomsen, no single person has ever had a greater positive effect on my life. You've always been there for me with honesty, support, and the best memories I've ever created. Thank you to everyone involved in the creation of HoxieConsulting.com and Hoxie Consulting. Thank you to Rick Caldwell and NorthEastMMA.net for showing me that my best contributions to MMA can be made outside of the ring.

Thank yous are due for a variety of reasons to so many people who have touched my life. Some of you know how important you are, and some may not even realize the effect you've had on my life. These people include, but are not limited to, Dan Sulitka and family, Ernesto Rivera, Jim McGowan and family, Matt and Pat Taranto, Dan Malay and family, Allison Marrero, Lisa Collins, Chris Byck, Joe and Terry Nastri, Fred and Kate Thomsen, Caithlin Lopes, John Hagopian, Tom Caulter, Charlie Ryan, Gavin Somics, David Rice and family, Peter Francis Alexander, Mom, Dad, God, and Trent Reznor.

About the Author

Mark Hoxie began his professional career as an advertising sales representative for the Yellow Pages in Los Angeles. Within his first year, he was one of the top salespeople on the entire West Coast. After finding similar success in print, newspaper, radio, television, Internet, and direct-mail marketing, he returned to his hometown of Syracuse, New York, to save his family's ailing business. Using his newfound expertise, he brought the business back from the ashes.

Currently, Mark is helping small and medium-sized businesses develop marketing strategies through his company, Hoxie Consulting. He has real-world experience sitting on both sides of the table—as an advertising sales representative and as a small business owner. Drawing from these experiences, he has helped hundreds of businesses grow and prosper. Mark also holds workshops and seminars for small business groups, schools, and advertising sales teams. To learn more, visit www.HoxieConsulting.com.

Contents

Chapter 4
Advertising Mediums **29**

Chapter 5
Implementing a Marketing Strategy 61

Chapter 6
Sales Reps, Contracts, and Negotiations. 83

Chapter 7
Content and Offers 99

Chapter 9
Industry Specifics **139**

Chapter 10
Business Theory **167**

Chapter 11
New Businesses 183

Index 193

Introduction

To get a better understanding of the purpose of this book, let me tell you a bit about its creation. Almost 10 years ago, I moved to Los Angeles and got into the world of advertising sales. It was my first sales job of any kind, so I was excited to soak up any knowledge I could find along the way. I quickly learned to uncover the needs of my potential customers and provide them with solutions. This kind of honest sales approach led me to become one of my company's top salespeople on the West Coast.

I developed an obsession with advertising. Have you ever had a Yellow Pages sales rep tell you, "No one ever just picks up the Yellow Pages to read them for fun"? They haven't met Mark Hoxie.

My thirst for knowledge led me from one advertising medium to another. I worked in television, radio, direct mail—you name it, I've sold it. Each time I changed positions, I would consult my sales team on how to sell against and, more importantly, in unison with other products. I had old customers calling me with marketing questions on a daily basis. I had several begging me to work for them full time as some version of a marketing director. Needless to say, I developed a bit of an ego.

My ego was quickly put in check when I learned my father was going to close down the family business back on the East Coast. He'd been in the painting business for almost 30 years and simply was no longer able to make ends meet. The market had changed, other businesses began to undercut him, and he was ready to hang it up. Without much hesitation, I gave up my life as an advertising sales executive in Los Angeles to try to save the family business back in Syracuse. Using my experience selling advertising and growing other people's businesses, I knew I could turn the company around.

After a complete marketing overhaul, I was able to raise the business from the ashes and bring it back to its former glory.

The advertising itch quickly caught up with me. There's nothing I love more than helping businesses grow through effective marketing and advertising, so I decided to turn the painting business over to my brother and get into consulting.

It didn't take me long to realize that I was out of my league. Most of the advertising consultants I could find had extensive resumes littered with Fortune 500 experience and high-end degrees and MBAs from some of the country's top universities. Others wrote books.

Because I don't have a fancy degree or experience with multinational corporations, I decided to take a shot at the latter option. I began to search local bookstores in an attempt to see what kind of books existed for small business marketing. Looking at the authors' qualifications, I felt like I hit another wall. These guys all had similar qualifications to the other consultants I had researched. They worked in marketing for huge national companies, and all of them had spent years obtaining various degrees and certifications.

And then it hit me like a ton of phonebooks: What do these guys know about marketing and advertising for *small* businesses? How can they draw any comparisons between marketing a national fast-food chain or automobile brand and the needs of small businesses operating solely in their own backyards?

As it turns out, they can't. The marketing strategies of a national electronics manufacturer have nothing to do with a florist trying to make a living. I've helped florists grow their business. I've also helped mechanics, lawyers, roofers, accountants, restaurants, and all kinds of other businesses have great success in local and regional markets. Most importantly, I helped saved my family's business.

I pitched this idea to an acquisitions editor at Cengage Learning, and she was sold. Cengage has an excellent series of books dedicated to helping businesses and professionals take on real-world challenges in 90 days, and a marketing and advertising book was a good fit.

The book you're holding in your hands does not have any get-rich-quick options. I'm not going to tell you how to advertise for free, and I'm not going to spend the whole book telling you how to create a pretty logo. This book is designed to give you the tools to make educated marketing decisions that can help your business weather the tough times and even grow to new heights. Within 90 days, you will be able to implement a more effective marketing strategy and be certain that you are getting the most bang for your buck. You will learn the ins and outs of various mediums and how to determine which advertising routes are best for your business.

Although this book is laid out in a linear, 90-day fashion, I encourage you to read the book thoroughly before making any decisions. After you have completed this book, hold onto it as a handy reference piece. Also, you will find that some of this book speaks to specific businesses or circumstances. Please consider them all. An accountant may learn something from the advice I give to restaurants. A well-established company could still pick up a few pointers from the new business section.

Just like investing in the market, investing in your own business requires certain financial risks. Please use this book as a tool to help you make more educated marketing investments. However, as you will hear me say throughout this entire book, always use your common sense.

I hope you learn a lot from this book and you are able to bring your business to a new level. Also, I've tried to keep this book upbeat and entertaining so that it doesn't drag on like some of the other books penned by far more worldly marketing "experts" sitting up in their high-rise offices. Growing your business doesn't have to be tedious—it should be an enjoyable experience.

So, enjoy!

Chapter 1

Why Advertise?

- What Is Advertising?
- Why Should You Advertise?
- New Businesses
- Objections
- Action Plan

Advertising makes the business world go round.

In a capitalistic free market society, every single business can benefit from proper marketing of their product or service. No matter how many referrals or repeat customers you have, no matter how obscure or mainstream your company is, advertising should be an integral part of your business plan.

Without any kind of marketing or advertising, it would be extremely difficult for consumers to make their buying decisions. Something as simple as getting your carpets cleaned would become a tedious task. Phonebooks wouldn't exist without advertising, so there goes calling a bunch of carpet cleaners. Much of the Internet would be non-existent without advertising, so forget about finding carpet cleaners there. Without any signage advertising businesses, you couldn't even wander the streets in search of their service! Consumers rely on advertisements to introduce and direct them to businesses that can fill their buying needs.

You've likely figured out that businesses rely on advertising to compete with their rivals. You might be the finest jeweler in town, but you're not going to capitalize on the Valentine's Day season if you're not out there advertising with your competition! All forms of advertising operate like salespeople by amplifying your message to the masses. More often than not, advertising can reach far more people for far less money than a salesperson can. Advertising then maximizes your salespeople's abilities because leads have been warmed up by your marketing reach.

What Is Advertising?

Anything that promotes your business can be considered advertising.

Advertising is simply anything that promotes your business. Most people understand that newspaper ads and television commercials are forms of advertising in the traditional sense. However, your signs, business cards, and even word-of-mouth referrals can be considered forms of advertising. It's important to balance a healthy mix of mediums to get the best results for your business.

Some advertising is used simply to keep your name out there at the front of people's minds so that when they are ready to make a buying decision, they think of you. This is called *branding*, and it can deliver long-lasting results. Other forms of advertising incite people to come in right away with an offer. These call-to-action ads can give your business an immediate boost in clientele.

Why Should You Advertise?

Customers and clients are the lifeblood of any small business. As a new business owner, you must do things to drive people to your business. Word of mouth is a great way to drum up business, but if you have not been around long enough to build a referral base, you need another source of customers. Advertising is quite simply the only way to drive new clients to your business. If all you had to do for the phone to magically begin to ring off the hook was open a business, everyone would be doing it.

If you're a new business owner, advertising is the only way to bring new clients to your business.

People who have been in business for some time can still benefit greatly from a marketing program. They may want to expand and may need extra sources of income to do so. Some existing business owners may want to focus on one of their primary goods or services. An effective marketing strategy can help them reach those goals.

Some people are reluctant to advertise because it is not a tangible purchase. When you buy a printer, you end up with a machine in your office that can print out documents. When you cut a check to the utility company, it's for the amount of energy your business consumed.

Advertising is different. When you buy an ad in a newspaper, what are you really getting? How many people look at your advertisement? How many come right in for a purchase? How many visit you way down the road? How many totally ignore it?

It's extremely difficult to quantify what you're getting when you purchase an ad. There are many ways to track your return, but this variable scares many business owners out of taking the advertising plunge. Worse yet, some people decide to just get their feet wet, which usually leads to weak results and the assumption that advertising doesn't work.

The more educated you are about marketing your type of business in your area, the more you can erase some of the uncertainty that comes with buying advertising. What works for a mattress dealer in Manhattan may not work for a dog groomer in a suburb of Minneapolis.

New Businesses

Businesses need to focus on marketing and advertising at their inception more than at any other point in their existence. For the most part, no one knows about your business yet. You may have some friends and family ready to give you business, but if you want to grow, you must advertise your products and services. Even if you are an expert at what you do and know that referrals will carry you on to the success you seek, you still need to build a customer base.

There's no need to start your business with baby steps. Hit the ground running with an effective marketing strategy.

There is a common misconception that you have to grow your business slowly and that it takes years to build a successful business. With the proper marketing strategy, you can hit the ground running. You certainly can take the slow route and learn to grow cautiously, but there's nothing stopping you from reaching as many people as you possibly can in a short period of time. We will discuss these specific strategies later in the book, but it's important for you to throw out the idea of taking little steps. If you do not commit to a substantial marketing strategy, you will likely fizzle out from the lack of income. A substantial part of your startup money *must* be directed at marketing.

I've heard many people suggest you should make sure you have enough money to cover your overhead for a year. However, covering rent, payroll, utilities, and other fixed bills for a year has nothing to do with bringing in new customers. I would rather new business owners roll the dice a bit and shorten that timeframe to three months but include a highly effective marketing plan that can immediately bring in income.

You can accomplish these lofty goals as long as you make smart buying decisions when it comes to your advertising. If you just blindly overspend on your marketing, you may not get the results you need to keep your business operating.

Objections

Although I will spend much of this book helping you overcome your objections to advertising, here is a quick back and forth that may shine some light on doubts you've had as a business owner. Also, because I'm not trying to sell you anything, I can be a little bolder with you than most advertising sales reps are willing to be.

"Advertising simply does not work!"

Do you really think that advertising sales reps are so good that they've been able to trick people into buying ads with their medium? What about that guy you've seen running the same ad for years? Do you think he just wants to be nice to his sales rep? Advertising has been around forever in all kinds of forms because it *can* work.

"But advertising didn't work for me/my friend/my family member in the past."

Chances are, you're the one who failed at advertising—advertising did not fail you. Did you run your ad long enough for people to notice it? Were you advertising in the best medium for your market and business type? Was your offer strong enough to call people to action? Did you only try getting your feet wet and run such a small program that no one noticed?

Don't worry; I'm not placing all the blame on business owners, because you likely trusted your sales rep. Your rep may have pointed you in the wrong direction or may have just taken your sale like an order, simply to do business with you.

"I ran several good-sized ads for a year, and they didn't work!"

How do you know? It's possible that they didn't, but how well do you track your customers? Did they all fail you, or was it just a few of them? Chances are, you don't know. Again, it can be difficult to track your results, but it's important to do everything you can to figure out what is working best for you. Some advertising methods, such as coupons, are easy to track, whereas some branding types of advertising are much more difficult to track. With a proper balance of tracking and education of your market, you can figure out what works best for you.

"But I already have enough business."

If you're truly working to your capacity, you're leaving money on the table. Either you need to expand or you need to raise your prices. Chances are, you're picking up this book to grow, so I doubt you'll turn down the added business advertising will bring in.

"I don't have room in my budget for advertising."

All day long, your sales reps are going to tell you, "If I could give you a $20 bill for every $5 bill you gave me, would you find room in your budget?" On a large scale, they're correct. Advertising is not a sucking hole in your budget meant to eat up your operating capital; it's an investment. Whether the salesperson sitting across the desk from you is the one to make that investment with is a whole other story....

"Okay, I'll take the smallest ad they have."

If you had a chunk of your leg chewed off by a lion, you wouldn't put a band-aid on it. But if you did, and band-aids were the only perception of medical treatment you had, you'd assume the medical world was a hoax, because obviously that band-aid wouldn't be of much help. If you were properly treated with bandages, emergency surgery, and proper rehabilitation, you'd trust the advice of medical professionals. Advertising is similar to (albeit slightly less painful than) this example. You will not be able to meet your marketing goals by going with the smallest or the cheapest way out. Small ads may work for certain businesses in certain circumstances, but it's important to identify your goals so that your marketing strategy can help you get there.

"People don't trust companies that advertise."

It's understandable that consumers may approach advertising with a little bit of hesitancy. They're afraid of "too good to be true" offers or claims. This is why it's important to be honest with your content. If you've been in business for more than 30 years, it's okay to share that with your potential clients. When you tell people they can get something free with their purchase, but then you change the stipulations of the offer once they get through the door, you're the one who caused the breach in trust. Although many people do in fact approach advertisements with hesitancy, the reality is that they still do approach them.

"I don't need to advertise, because I do all my business on referrals."

Great! It sounds as if you do such a great job that people like to refer you to their friends, family, and business associates. Why not add more clients to that referral base? If you have an easy time getting referrals, the clients you bring in via advertising are worth exponentially more. One new call from an ad could lead to several more customers via referrals. As a good entrepreneur, you don't need a huge response to turn your leads into more business. People who churn and burn their customers need to advertise more to replace their dwindling and disappointed customer base. They stay around status quo, while you can grow your clientele at an exponential rate.

"People who are swayed by advertising are shoppers looking for deals and low prices."

You're right; many times they are. But how will they ever consider you if they never see your business's marketing? Maybe your prices aren't the lowest in town, but maybe they're better than the one or two businesses people are comparing them to. Also, if you don't want those kinds of customers, don't advertise to them! Focus on the exclusivity of your business, and the frugal shoppers will stay away while the people willing to pay more for legitimate quality will come calling. Just remember, even people with more to spend like a deal.

"I don't want to make an offer or include a coupon because I can't afford it and/or I don't want to seem cheap and miss out on big-ticket customers!"

If you don't have enough of a margin to make deals or offers, your prices are too low to begin with. Secondly, do you think people with high income and money to spend don't want a deal? The reality is that most people who have that kind of money look for deals and have good financial sense. Don't be afraid to draw them in with a deal, even though you're still more expensive than your competition after the discount!

"Times are tough, and we have to cut our expenses."

You think times are tough now? Wait until you see what happens if you cut your advertising! There is always room to trim the fat when times are lean, but just like you wouldn't stop paying the electric bill, you can't stop paying for advertising. Either way, the lights will be going out.... By easing off on branding and focusing on calls to action, you can make immediate sales to get through the tough times.

"Okay, sign me up!"

Whoa there! As much as your advertising sales rep would love to hear that, it's important that you negotiate and visit with as many salespeople from as many mediums as possible. Later on in this book, I'll teach you how to figure out what is right for your business and how to go out and get it at a reasonable price.

So why will this book help you? Building an effective marketing strategy is a lot like playing a game of poker. As a business owner, you may have your guard up, and you may not want to share your hand with the steady stream of salespeople who solicit you on a daily basis. They will be playing the same game. They don't want to show you their weaknesses and bottom-line pricing, and they especially don't want to lose you to their competition. It's your goal to learn as much as you can about your opponent so that you can play your hand accordingly and win at the game of advertising.

As someone who has both sold advertising and worked as a business owner buying advertising, I can share with you the ins and outs that most people have to learn through trial and error. Consider me the person standing behind your poker opponent, telling you what cards he's holding!

The reality is that you can build a mutually beneficial relationship with your advertising sales reps. You can achieve your marketing goals, and they can hit their sales numbers.

This book will also help you to get a better understanding of what different mediums can do for your business. Billboards and coupon magazines can do different things for different businesses. Your friend who runs a car dealership may do well with television ads, but as an accountant, the same program would not work for you.

My goal is to help you educate yourself on your local market and build an effective marketing strategy within a 90-day window. It may seem like a short amount of time to revamp your business's current marketing plan, but you will learn that immersing yourself in advertising for just a few months will pay off exponentially. When you have a solid handle on your marketing strategy, you'll be able to spend less time planning how to increase your business and more time dealing with your growing clientele!

Action Plan

This initial action plan will help you make better sense of the later chapters. If you can answer these questions and then keep them at the front of your mind, you'll be on the right track to creating a new and more effective marketing strategy for your business. Gather your current advertising marketing and materials and ask yourself these questions:

✓ What led you to make these marketing decisions?

✓ What ways have you tracked your results in the past?

✓ What problems have you had with advertising in the past?

✓ If your business is newer, what forms of marketing have you already visualized for your company?

✓ How do you plan on generating your initial sales?

Chapter 2

Identifying Your Business

- Determining Quality versus Quantity
- Identifying Your Prime Products and Services
- Knowing Your Competition
- Knowing Your Local Market
- Acknowledging Your Limits and Potential
- Setting Your Goals
- Action Plan

Identifying your business is likely the most important and most overlooked aspect of building a successful advertising campaign. Sure, you may already know that you're a plumber or a dentist, but what kind of business are you trying to run? It is important for you to take an honest look at your business so you can create a realistic and effective image. The clearer the picture you paint of your business, the easier it will be for you to identify and attract your ideal customers and clients.

Determining Quality versus Quantity

The first and simplest way to break down your business is by quality and quantity. Does your business plan involve being profitable by conducting a high volume of business, or are your margins going to be bigger because you are delivering a high-quality product or service? Each of these styles is to be respected, and both have their pluses and minuses. However, the one consistent factor they share is that either type of business can benefit from effective advertising.

If your business is to be known for its quality, it is expected that you may not have the lowest prices in town. It may limit the customer pool you are drawing from, but it will generally allow you to make more profit per transaction. Of course there is a ceiling to your prices, but your customers expect to receive the best product or service available.

You can be known for high quality or for competitive pricing. It's essential to recognize which one is the goal of your business so you can create effective advertising.

If your business is to be known for low prices, your customer base will likely be wider and willing to give up some quality for a better price. Although you may have a lower profit margin per transaction, you can make it up through volume of business. Remember, though, even with a discount product or service, your customers will expect some level of quality—especially if you want their continued business.

It is important for you to figure out which of these two categories your business falls into so that your advertisements can bring you the kind of clients you are looking for. Many people try to market their business as having the best product or service at the lowest prices. As a business owner, you know that accomplishing something like that is virtually impossible, and most consumers understand that as well. No one goes into a Mercedes dealership expecting to find Hyundai prices. At the same time, no one purchases a Kia expecting it to handle like a BMW. This is not to say that your business is restricted to quality or quantity; rather, it is to get you on track for an effective marketing strategy.

Sometimes, different revenue streams within your business may have different types of profitability. As an auto mechanic, you may do dozens of brake jobs per day at a lower margin, but you make more money per job repairing diesel engines. Knowing the differing profit types within your business can help you market them independently. This same mechanic would likely benefit from a highly circulated coupon for brakes. He could then also run a specialized technical ad about diesel repair in a local business-to-business publication.

When a business is concerned with volume and bringing in a high number of sales, price is usually the best feature for your advertising to target. Regardless of the mediums in which you choose to advertise, you can stick with statements such as "Lowest Prices in Town" or "We'll Beat Any Competitor's Price." Stay away from featuring quality, or else you might scare away the budget-minded buyer while likely not delivering for the people truly seeking quality.

If your business is concerned with quality, the opposite is true. Feature the quality of your product, your reputation, and any other aspect of your company that makes you better than your competition. Although offers to get people in the door are okay, stay away from making price the focal point of your ads.

Identifying Your Prime Products and Services

How many times have you seen an ad for a contractor who does it all? Roofing, siding, foundations, windows, drywall, electrical, and more! The more your company can offer to the consumer, the more revenue sources your business stands to benefit from. However, it is important for you to focus your message when seeking out potential clients. If you were looking for a roofer in a home improvement magazine, would you call the firm with 25 bullet points denoting services they offer, or would you pay more attention to the ad featuring roofing? Although you may offer multiple products or services, it is important to focus on your most profitable or most frequently needed product or service. Once you get your customers "through the door," they can be exposed to the other benefits of conducting business with your company. There are many venues where it is important to list what you offer (such as the Yellow Pages), but it is still important to limit the specific business you are going to seek out.

The same self-reflection can help when determining what kinds of offers you are going to make to your potential customers. For example, pet-store owners may choose to advertise in a coupon mailer where they can list many of their products or services. However, instead of a generalized coupon offering 10 percent off any product or service, they will have better results with specific offers. Specific offers elicit a stronger response from consumers with specific needs. A coupon for $15 off grooming will inspire a specific action and draw the consumer to one of their more profitable services. If the pet-store owner was looking for more volume, an aggressive offer for a basic need, such as pet food, would drive up the store's traffic and retail sales.

Focus your advertising on your prime products and services. If you try to include every product or service you offer in an ad, you'll lose people's interest. Keep it simple and straightforward for best results.

The other benefit to specific offers is that you can draw people to the specific part of your business you are trying to increase. Using the pet-store example, if grooming is a particularly profitable part of the business, then a coupon specifically for grooming is a good way to increase business in that area. A generalized coupon for 10 percent off any service is vague—it doesn't tell customers that the store specializes in grooming as one of their services.

Since an effective advertising campaign will cover more than one medium, you can certainly focus on improving more than one piece of your business. Landscapers could use television ads to display the beautiful fish ponds they specialize in, but they may also choose to run a newspaper ad promoting lawn maintenance. If those same landscapers tried to cover every service they offered in their television commercial, their message would be cluttered. If they tried to do the same in a newspaper, they would likely lose the reader's attention. The results would be little increase in their business, as people would likely ignore the television ad or skip over the print ad.

The most profitable part of your business is likely the part you would prefer to increase. However, simply advertising this one feature is not always the best route. It is important to focus on some of your more common services to get more people exposed to your business. Once they have a certain comfort level or even uncover a need that you are able to fill, you will have an opportunity for an up-sell. An insurance agent may want to sell life policies more than anything else, but auto may be the thing that first draws customers in. If you understand what type of business you are running and which aspects will bring people through the door, you're on your way to a successful marketing strategy.

Knowing Your Competition

All businesses face varying forms of competition. It is important for you to become familiar with your competition so you can compare and contrast your products and services. Knowing the difference between you and other similar businesses will help you to market your business more competitively. Ask yourself the following questions:

- **How do your prices compare?** A grocer who feels his ground beef is a deal at $4.99 per pound would be ill-advised to advertise that if everyone else is offering it at $3.99 per pound. Instead, his $1.99 gallon of milk may be a better draw if it's less expensive than the competition's.

- **How does your quality compare?** Sticking with our grocer example, a better way for the grocer to market his pricier beef would be to highlight its quality. Mentioning in a radio commercial organic, grass-fed, certified Angus beef ground fresh daily may bring in people looking for a higher-quality burger.

- **What are you offering that no one else can?** Maybe this grocer has an exclusive agreement with an ostrich farmer in the region. He would certainly benefit from making his access to this unique product known to the public.

Advertising exists because of competition. If Dianne was the only accountant in town, people looking for an accountant would have to go to her unless they wanted to travel. She would have little need to advertise, given that she's the only choice available. However, if Joe the accountant moved to town and started to advertise discount tax returns, Dianne would certainly lose business. Not wanting to change her prices, she might choose to advertise her high tax refunds and her reputation for accuracy. If you know your competition, you will know how to effectively compete and market your business.

Knowing your competition also means knowing your competition's marketing strategies. There are a variety of reasons to pay close attention to their advertisements. Ask yourself:

- **Where is your competition advertising?** If most of your local competitors are placing ads in the PennySaver, you need to have a presence as well. An abundance of similar businesses appearing in the same publication is likely due to a high success rate within your market. Also, if consumers are trained to look in this publication for your service, and you are not there, don't expect them to go looking for you elsewhere. Keep in mind, too, that because of the high amount of competition within this publication, it is important for you to have a strong offer or something that sets you apart from the other advertisers.

- **Where aren't your competitors advertising?** Sometimes, a medium with a lack of competition is a ripe place to find new business. If you find a church bulletin littered with dozens of advertisers, but none of them owns a funeral home, like you do, it may be a good place to advertise. At the same time, you have to use common sense. There may be no funeral homes advertising on Nickelodeon, but that's the case for a reason. There are better places to find your demographic.

- **What are the big players doing?** It may be cheap for all of the electricians in your area to run classified ads, but what are the big players doing? If there is a company that you strive to emulate or compete with, it's a good idea to pay specific attention to their plan. If the top electrician in town is everywhere you look on television, that might be a great place to go head to head. However, if you've already determined that your business is not out to compete directly with his, then avoiding television commercials altogether might be a safer bet.

Outside of advertising, it is a good idea to know what your competition is doing to make sure you are keeping up with the industry standards. Just as you don't want to be left in the dust with regard to your marketing, the same can be said about any aspect of your business. Becoming familiar with your competition lets you know who you're up against, but knowing your local market allows you to see what all small businesses are doing as a whole.

Knowing Your Local Market

Beyond your own competition, it is a good idea to identify what other businesses are doing in your local market. If there is a particular Yellow Pages directory that has almost every other business doing something more than a free listing, it is a good idea for you to have a presence as well. Businesses like to advertise where they will get a response. I know it sounds like a simplified idea, but if everyone is doing it, everyone is benefitting. It's highly unlikely that an advertising sales force has duped the entire business community into advertising in a publication that simply does not work. Consumers also tend to look to whatever medium has the most businesses present when they are ready to make a buying decision. Keeping these trends in mind, you'll be able to build a better marketing strategy.

Acknowledging Your Limits and Potential

It is important to know your company's limits as well as your own personal limits. If there is something your business cannot deliver because of its size or resources, you need to be upfront and honest with your customers when you are advertising. If you are a painting contractor with two employees, you cannot advertise quick or immediate services. There may be a point when you are booked out two months in advance and simply cannot keep up and offer immediate service. With only two employees, you are also not going to be able to paint an apartment building as fast as a firm with multiple crews and more employees. Knowing this, you are better off advertising that the owner is on the premises at all times and leave the speedy service to someone else. False advertising may get you the job initially, but you will ruin your reputation quickly if you cannot deliver.

Know your limits and always make sure your advertising is truthful about what you can accomplish for your customers.

One of the advantages of owning your own business is being your own boss. If you have personal limits, do not be afraid to limit what you offer. If you value your family time or you want somewhat of a normal schedule, do not offer 24-hour service! Sure, you will get more business because some people may need you at midnight, but if you over-market yourself, you will end up doing things you never wanted to do in the first place.

Your business's capabilities should help dictate your advertising and marketing strategies.

Not all small businesses are small. Maybe as a painting contractor, you have 35 employees spread out over six crews. You may be able to offer to take on all jobs within a week of acceptance, or you might be able to finish most houses in less than three days. Don't be afraid to flex your business muscles and show what your company is really capable of! At the same time, don't advertise, "No job too small" if you're not willing to spend your time doing an estimate for one room or a garage door.

Knowing your business's limits and potential will also help you establish how much advertising you should do. The painter with two employees may get a lot of calls from primetime television commercials, full-page newspaper ads, and weekly direct mailings to every homeowner in the region, but chances are he could not take on all the work (or pay for all his advertising). At the same time, another painting contractor may find his 35 employees looking for things to do if he only has a bold listing in the Yellow Pages and a do-it-yourself website.

Setting Your Goals

Identifying your business's goals is another key factor in determining your advertising.

As a business owner, it is important to have goals to set the tone for your marketing strategies. If you're a new business owner, it's essential to get your name out there and get your foot in the door to start building a reputation. What kind of reputation do you want to build? Maybe you've been in business for a while. Are you looking to increase your overall business? Would you prefer to focus on one of the more profitable or enjoyable aspects of your business? Is it time to grow or time to downsize? Is there a certain season or sale you want to focus on? Setting goals can help dictate how much and what type of advertising you should consider.

No matter what your goals are, the proper advertising plan can help you to accomplish them. Once you have identified your own business and made your goals clear to yourself, the following chapters can be used to help you effectively accomplish whatever you have set out to do.

Action Plan

The following chapters will break down the various forms of media available in most markets. We will also talk about offers, competition, implementation, and tracking. Answering these questions will help you take away more from the following chapters while putting you on the right track to finding success in marketing and advertising your small business in 90 days.

✓ Does your overall business plan focus on volume or quality?

✓ Do your individual revenue streams focus on volume or quality?

✓ What is your most profitable product or service?

✓ What is your most frequently sought product or service?

✓ What do you do better or cheaper than your competition?

✓ Where is your competition advertising?

✓ Where is the rest of the market advertising?

✓ How much work are you willing and able to take on?

✓ What are your goals?

Chapter 3

Identifying Your Customers

- Demographics
- Typical versus Prime
- Tracking Your Customer Base
- Buying Habits
- Knowing Your Neighborhoods
- High-End Failures
- Action Plan

Identifying your customers is the number-one way to streamline your advertising. By knowing who your best and most frequent customers are, where to find them, and how to attract them, you can maximize your advertising dollar.

Demographics

With today's technology, it has become easier than ever to target certain demographics. Also, demographics as applied to advertising are no longer limited to age, gender, and income range. Some research companies can give you population breakdowns based on hobbies, types of pets, and even people's weights!

Companies of all sizes can benefit from using demographics, as similar people tend to make similar buying decisions. For example, women over the age of 50 living in a house worth more than $500,000 will likely make the same kinds of purchases when you look at them as a large group. And men under the age of 25 living in apartments would have a completely different set of buying habits from the aforementioned women over 50.

When you are able to identify your customer base, this data can serve a much more useful purpose. You can use demographic data as a tool when choosing mediums in which to advertise. It may turn out that your targeted demographic reads a certain section of the newspaper, or maybe they have a very specific cable station they're loyal to. It's important to truly pay attention to your market and not make assumptions about what customers you want to attract. Breaking down demographics will do nothing for you unless you properly identify your customers.

Typical versus Prime

Typical customers tend to have more frequent, smaller transactions with you. Prime customers have fewer transactions, but those they do have are on a larger scale.

It is important to differentiate between your typical and prime customers. These classifications are not in regard to customers' demographics; rather, they deal with the type of business customers conduct with you.

Typical customers make the most frequent purchases or transactions with you. For a mechanic, typical customers might be those who need brake jobs. For a florist, typical customers might be those who order a dozen roses.

Prime customers are usually less frequent, but they're the ones you love to see walking through the door or calling you on the phone. That same mechanic might prefer prime customers buying brand-new transmissions, while the florist is waiting for that bride-to-be.

Sometimes, your typical customers can become prime customers. It's important to bring in and satisfy your typical customers so that when they're ready to make a larger buying decision (thus becoming a prime customer), they will come to you once again.

One of the biggest mistakes an advertiser can make is "elephant hunting." If you're a new real-estate agent, and you claim to be the expert in selling multimillion-dollar homes, but you're not addressing your most frequent type of customers, you're going to miss a lot of opportunity. If your ad in a local magazine shows a stock photo of a $10 million home, you may not get a call from the family trying to sell their ranch home on the other side of town. A better idea is to have a quick blurb about servicing all ranges of clients, but focusing your ad on service and things that get you more calls. After selling 10 average homes, not only will you have made some money, but maybe you will also have built a positive relationship with someone who's aunt is looking to sell her million-dollar home.

Tracking Your Customer Base

Regardless of whether you're dealing with typical or prime customers, it's important to get to know your customers. Identifying similar traits in clients you like (or dislike) can help you reach similar people in your local market. For example, if you are a furniture dealer, you might prefer clients who purchase complete sets as opposed to individual pieces. You may spend a good amount of money sending direct mail to the most affluent neighborhood in your town, assuming that those customers are most likely to purchase furniture sets instead of individual pieces. However, by tracking your customers' ZIP codes and buying habits, you might find that a middle-class neighborhood on the other side of town sends the real big-ticket shoppers through your doors. Or, maybe you'll find that seniors purchase the most furniture sets, or families with three or more children, and so on.

When you've identified your customers' buying traits, you can better target your customers with your advertising.

As you begin to paint a picture of the demographics you prefer, you can start targeting your customers more effectively. If you're an optometrist, it may turn out that seniors are your best clients. Because their demographic still tends to heavily favor the Yellow Pages, a sharp ad (with large print) in your local directory might be a good idea. You might also like getting first-time eyeglass-wearers through the door, so an effective social-marketing tool with local doctors may get you the new referrals you need. Be sure to have a profile with any of these mainstream sites for social purposes, but don't be afraid to use it to link up with your targeted audience.

Making these moves based on your customer demographic will save you money over canvassing the entire population. Over-marketing a population can weaken your advertising dollar if only a certain percentage of people will be doing business with you.

Creating a tracking system for your customers will help you build a customer profile while also tracking your individual advertising results. If your information is thorough enough, you can also build mailing lists from it. Don't be afraid to get as much information from your customers as they will comfortably give up! Addresses, email addresses, phone numbers, age, gender, occupation, family members, home ownership, and feedback are all things you should keep track of.

You don't have to obtain all these bits of detail on a customer query form. Casually ask about the person's occupation and family members if the conversation allows. You can also obtain some of this information (address, phone number, email address) by using your order forms or online questionnaires.

Buying Habits

It's fairly easy to track details such as names and addresses of your customers. But it is also crucial to track your customers' buying habits. Not only can this information help you with your marketing, it can also help you during the sales process. If you sell motorcycles and apparel, you may notice that your customers who buy the prime bike you want to sell also have an enormous interest in certain riding gloves. In your next newspaper ad, why not offer a free pair of gloves with any new bike purchase?

As individual as people are, the human decision-making process tends to be distinct. If you're a financial planner and you find that the people who buy life insurance from you also tend to invest the most into stocks and mutual funds, try featuring your insurance policies in your advertisements. You'll get people in for a basic sale, but you'll also have the opportunity to expand into other services with a well-targeted client.

In the previous chapter, you learned that it is important to identify your style of business. The purpose of identifying your business is so that you are able to mesh better with your clientele. If you own a discount-flooring center, but all of your buyers are coming in seeking high-end tile, one of two things may be happening. First and most likely, you are marketing your business as something it is not. Your flashy television ad may show beautiful installed floors, but when people come into your showroom, they see stacks of flooring scattered about in a warehouse fashion and handwritten price tags with red slashes everywhere. There is a place for a business like that, but you're bringing in customers with buying habits that don't match what you're providing.

The second possibility is that there's a gap in the local supply-and-demand chain. These customers may have nowhere else to go for high-end tile—or at least they're not hearing anyone's marketing message. In this case, there's less to change with your marketing program and more opportunity that you should consider in your business plan.

> Don't be afraid to change your business plan if you find a new and lucrative opportunity!

Buying habits also have a lot to do with what drives people to make a buying decision. Some people are coupon shoppers; others prefer designated sales events. A buy-one-get-one-free coupon may work for some shoe stores, while others might find more success with a buy-one-get-one-free weekend event. Trial and error with both of these methods will teach you what works best, but only if you pay attention to your results!

Some people want cutting-edge services and products, and others favor tradition. You may own a couple of carwashes, but what is it that brings people in? Do they like flashy machines and eco-friendly cleaning products, or do they come for the old-fashioned hand drying at the end? Obviously people come for the wash itself, but knowing what aspect of the business draws them in will help you build the content of your advertisements. Know your customers' buying habits, and you're one step closer to creating a successful ad campaign.

There are multiple ways to extend the same basic offer to your customers. Find out which one they best respond to and use that angle in your advertising.

If you are actively in business now, it's also important to figure out what kinds of offers your customers respond to best. I've always been a fan of offering dollar values off the purchase price or FREE incentives with my painting company. I've used $600 off any job over $4,000, and I've offered free deck staining with any full exterior paint jobs. You may find that offering a certain percentage off your price or a buy-one-get-one situation works best. It just depends what your customers respond to best.

I could have said 15-percent off any job over $4,000, which is virtually the same offer, but after my own trial-and-error tests, I found that my customer base favored cash values and free offers. Some people just like seeing published prices. I've known other painting contractors to have success with $200 per room or $1,995 total for a single-level exterior paint job. Figuring out what your customers prefer can help you set the agenda for all of your advertised offers.

Beyond offers, you also need to figure out what qualities draw people to your business. As an attorney, you may offer free consultations, but likely everyone else does, too. So why do people choose to do business with you? Do they feel comfortable because you're a third-generation attorney? Do they get drawn in by testimonials? Don't be afraid to flat-out ask what drew your customer in. If he or she liked that you're a third-generation attorney, and you've heard the same thing a dozen times, consider featuring this point in your print or online ads.

Knowing Your Neighborhoods

On a local level, it may be difficult to find demographic data from neighborhood to neighborhood or even between ZIP codes. Some direct-mailing agencies can scour for data, but that can't beat general familiarity. If you're not a longtime resident of your city or region, take some time to get out and familiarize yourself with different neighborhoods. It may seem fruitless to drive aimlessly through your town, but with a keen eye you can learn a lot about different population pockets within your own region.

You might be surprised to see three dry cleaners on the same street in a small suburb. Maybe you never realized there was a historic-homes district right in the middle of a sea of apartment buildings. College kids may have taken over an area you once associated with large families. Maybe a new shopping plaza has sprung up on the far end of town, or another has completely closed its doors.

Paying attention to all of these changes and details on a local level can help you better tailor your advertising program. Placing a billboard ad for your pool-installation service by an off ramp leading toward student housing makes about as much sense as sending direct mail about your new paintball park to a senior-living community. Different advertising mediums break up your region in different ways, so it's important to really know your area. You can vary your message from area to area based on who is paying attention and what you want them to take away from your advertisement.

The previous two examples were obviously somewhat comical, but what if you changed the message? The pool-installation billboard toward all the student housing could read, "Hey, professors! How are YOU spending your summer?" and feature a picture of a beautifully installed pool. The direct mailing to a senior community about a paintball park could read, "Get your grandchildren what they REALLY want this year! An all-day pass to our park!" Knowing who you are speaking to can drive your message.

High-End Failures

Many advertisers make the mistake of over-marketing wealthier areas. Sure, people with million-dollar homes may have amassed a fortune over their lives, but that says nothing about their spending habits. If anything, it may show that they hold on even tighter to their dollars. One of the richest men I've ever known still cuts his own hair!

Wealthy doesn't necessarily mean big spender.

People who have carefully held onto and grown their assets tend to make more calculated buying decisions and (unfortunately) are far less swayed by advertising to begin with. They often resort to connections and recommendations to meet their buying needs. People in lower income brackets are often less concerned with amassing capital and are willing to spend their money more freely. If your specialty is installing new countertops, your best bet is to do quality work for middle-class homeowners and gain the high-end tickets through referrals. If you dump your entire marketing campaign into imported Italian marble countertops, you're going to miss those bread-and-butter jobs, and you may not even get a single hit from a wealthy customer.

All of these factors are important to consider when an advertising representative is trying to get you to sign on the dotted line. While some reps are building their territory by selling effective advertising, many just try to get you to spend as much as they feel they can get out of you. This is why it's important to be educated about your customer base. You can learn a lot from your advertising reps, but the more you know about what you want, the less room they have to "sell."

Action Plan

To successfully and efficiently market and advertise your small business, you must identify your customers. Once you've done so, you will have an easier time implementing and tweaking your marketing strategy.

✓ Identify who your typical customers are. What are they buying, what is their demographic, and where are they coming from?

✓ Identify who your prime customers are. What are they buying, what is their demographic, and where are they coming from?

✓ Build a worksheet for tracking your customer base's demographics and buying habits.

✓ Become familiar with your local neighborhoods.

✓ Determine what kinds of offers your customers respond to.

✓ Find out why your customers choose to do business with you.

✓ Discover how businesses like yours have penetrated high-end markets.

Chapter 4

Advertising Mediums

- Yellow Pages
- Online Directories
- Web Ads
- Television
- Radio
- Newspaper
- Direct Mail
- Coupon Publications
- Local Magazines
- Billboards
- Signage and In-Store Marketing
- Social Networking: Online and Real Life
- Other Mediums
- Action Plan

Now that you have a better grasp on your own business and customer base, it's time to look at all of your advertising options. In later chapters we'll discuss how to build marketing programs and what works best for varying types of small businesses. Also, in later chapters we will talk about negotiating with advertising sales representatives from each of these mediums.

Yellow Pages

The Yellow Pages have long been considered the backbone of any strong advertising campaign. No matter how many billboards and television commercials you have, people are going to have to find your number once they're ready to make a buying decision. Although you can find most phone numbers online, many people still reach for this book when they need to place a call.

When the phone companies were deregulated, allowing competitive providers into the area, the Yellow Pages became a service that could be offered by any directory company. Most markets have at least two versions of Yellow Pages covering the area, but many highly populated areas, such as Los Angeles and Miami, have more than a dozen companies printing out Yellow Pages. Some directories are printed in different languages, while others may target specific populations.

Pay attention to the scope of the books you're considering. Some directories will "under scope" certain areas, giving the book a more local feel. Others will "over scope," covering a much wider area. Smaller directories are perfect for pizza restaurants or dry cleaners who usually serve smaller populations. Larger books are great for attorneys or contractors who are looking to reach out to a broader audience.

Pros

People consulting the Yellow Pages are ready to make buying decisions. Don't miss this opportunity!

Although some people feel the Yellow Pages are a thing of the past, most people agree that they will still be around in some form over the next two decades. Aging populations often favor directories because they're comfortable with them, and Yellow Pages directories will always be handy tools for emergency buyers. Also, the Yellow Pages can give a better sense of legitimacy to any local business. For better or worse, many consumers will assume that if you're in the Yellow Pages, you're not a fly-by-night company.

If you choose to pay for ads in a directory, it will give you the chance to go head to head with your competitors right in front of consumers' eyes. If someone is looking for a landscaper who can install ponds, and that's in your ad, the person will call you first. Having your listing under several different categories will also expose you to many avenues of income. A house-cleaning service has obvious headings to be listed under, but don't forget other headings, such as window cleaning, floor polishing, or any other heading in the book that may yield some calls for you.

Many advertisers feel that having a boastful ad will make their company come across as expensive. For this argument I have two responses. First of all, in the ad you can talk about your pricing being reasonable or competitive. And second, do you really want those buyers who are calling every listing in the book for the lowest price? People who pick up the Yellow Pages are ready to make a buying decision. This is your opportunity to sell yourself to potential buyers before you even meet them.

Cons

With multiple directories serving many areas, it can be difficult to know which directory will get the best results. After meeting with several salespeople, you'll find that they all have the numbers to back up their book as being number one. Depending on how the surveys were done and who was doing them, salespeople can play with the numbers to serve their agendas. Ask around and find out what book your friends, neighbors, and other business owners are using.

Many companies will try to couple your book advertising with an online version of their directory. They may try to strong-arm you into advertising online to give you better rates within the book. The reason they are pushing so hard for these online sales is because there is an enormous profit margin for online directories. After updating your listing on their site, there is little cost to them associated with keeping your number listed. And although many people are making the move to finding numbers online, these big companies are moving there at a much faster rate to improve their bottom line. Although being listed online is a good idea, make sure you're getting all of the discounts you are entitled to without jumping through all of your salesperson's hoops.

Yellow Pages ads are considered to be directional advertisements. Directional ads serve the purpose of directing people to a specific business or industry when they are actively ready to make a buying decision. People do not look through the directory casually, so there is not a lot of opportunity to inspire buying decisions. Although you should always be listed and should give serious consideration to paid advertisement, you will also need other forms of advertising to drive people to your business.

What Works?

When considering your Yellow Pages advertising, pay attention to what your competitors are doing in the directory.

The Yellow Pages offer a great range of products and pricing to fit any advertising budget. Minimally, you must be listed under your primary heading. Pay attention to what other advertisers are doing under your heading. If there are a few bold listings and in-column or text ads, there's no need to consider a large ad. Get the basics in there and make sure you include bullet points that show how you are different or better than your competitors.

If you're in a heading that's flooded with advertisers, such as lawyers or plumbers, you have a couple of options. If you're comfortable spending a good amount on a full-page ad, make sure you maximize your ad's effectiveness. This does *not* mean you should cram as much information in the ad as possible; it just means that you need to take time to develop a good ad with your representative.

Most reputable Yellow Pages will design and build your ad at no added cost. Highlight some of your major features to catch people's eyes when they're looking for a certain product or service. In a different section of your ad, list the general bullet points pertaining to your company. If you go for color, take advantage of it and include a pertinent photo.

Contrary to what your rep will tell you, your phone number does not need to be huge! The more space they fill up, the easier their job of building the ad becomes. Make sure your number is in an obvious place, such as at the bottom center of the ad, and just use color or a knock-out box to make it easy to find.

I know you have a lot of pride in your business, but taking up half your ad with your name is also not a very good use of space. People who are comparison shopping don't care who you are; they want to know what you offer. If they already were planning to call you, they'll be sure to find you.

If you're in a popular heading and you cannot bring yourself to spend the money that goes along with a large ad, consider building your ad around one of your top or more popular features. If you're a dentist who decides to go with a quarter-page ad and just list a few of the same bullet points as your competitors, you're going to be overlooked. Instead, focus on something that will lock in people looking for a specific need to be filled. If you're a root-canal specialist, feature that part of your business to draw in the people who may feel they need the extra attention. If you offer discount cleanings, don't be afraid to put a big $39.99 in the middle of your ad—or whatever your super discount is that you use to get people in the door.

The Yellow Pages are a slowly sinking industry. They will likely be around in some form for years to come, but they are suffering losses on a yearly basis. Dig deep for discounts, because they are there. The people who publish the Yellow Pages want their book to be full of ads to drive usage and their sales process, so they're willing to deal. When I was employed by an independent Yellow Pages, I worked with a flooring company who spent a considerable amount of money in a book that was not doing very well. Management wanted to sell the specialty items, so they were matching the dollar value of the back cover of the book with ads inside the book. I was able to basically throw in the outside back cover of the book for the price of the program they were going to buy either way in their headings.

A final note: Anything beyond a bold listing in the White Pages is a waste of money. You're making your number easier to find, but beyond that, people were already looking for your number to begin with, so there is no need to advertise to them.

SCAM ALERT

Watch out for generic bills in the mail from a "Yellow Pages" company. When the phone companies were deregulated, the black and yellow fingers became a public and non-trademarked icon that anyone can use. Some illegitimate companies will send businesses relatively small bills to be listed in nonexistent directories, expecting them to be paid without a thought.

Online Directories

As I stated earlier, many online directories are services offered in unison with printed Yellow Pages. Search engines can also be considered directories now that people can search on local levels.

Pros

Nowadays many people use the Internet to conduct business. Take advantage of this by creating a listing to use in online directories.

More and more people are using the Internet to conduct business online and offline. Sometimes the transactions take place purely online, and other times online persuasion is used to get people to make a buying decision offline with a local company. Most people have access to a computer or sit in front of one all day. When it's time for them to find a new hair salon or barber, they will likely use the tool in front of them to find a new provider. This can be advantageous to you, because all online directories can link people to your website or at least provide a large volume of information about your business.

Many people using smartphones and iPhones have Internet access as well. Now people can look up a number and dial it with the same device. Most of the major directories and search engines are highly compatible with these devices, but make sure to ask your sales rep to confirm their compatibility.

People from out of the area may be making buying decisions in your area for one reason or another. Travelers, adult children of local parents, people moving to your town—all would likely do their search for numbers online because they would have no access to any other form of local media.

Many online directories offer a pay-per-click service. This is when you offer an actual price for each click-through to your business's number or website. It is a great way to define a value for your leads and to make sure your online ad program is paid based on results.

Usually a business owner will set up a budget for any given month. Let's say he's willing to pay up to $300 per month, and he wants to pay 15 cents per click. In July, only 1,000 people click the ad, so the business owner is billed $150. Let's say November rolls around and seasonal business picks up. Now 2,000 people click on the ad, reaching the maximum budget of $300. The ad will no longer appear until the following month. Good online providers will usually notify you that you've reached your cap, just in case you'd like to expand your budget.

The price you pay per click depends on your business type. The higher the price you're willing to pay, the more often your ad will appear. This creates a bidding situation. A suit store paying 15 cents per click will show up ahead of or more often than another store bidding 5 cents per click. Someone else may come in and offer 20 cents per click to jump ahead of our first example. Your sales rep will give you the breakdown of the bidding so you can best assign a value for your click prices. Use your common sense. An accident attorney may need to pay more than a dollar per click, depending on a variety of situations and competition. A shoe repair company would likely be paying pennies.

If you're working with one of the larger companies out there, you don't have to worry about someone sitting in a dark room clicking your links to boost your bill all day long.

Cons

If you think there are a lot of Yellow Pages directories serving your area, there are hundreds more doing the same thing online. It can be difficult to know which ones will get you the most business. Although online ads are some of the easiest to track, they still cannot guarantee results. I listed my business with an online directory after learning that painting contractors in my area were searched for more than 300 times per month. I set up the ad to go to my cell phone instead of the main business line. Over the two-month course that I left my ad online, I didn't receive a single call. Please do not let this discourage you from advertising online; just remember that tracking and researching who you are advertising with is of the utmost importance.

It can be hard to get your toes wet with online advertising. If you're going to do it, you *must* have a decent website (though you should have one either way). You have to be sure to be listed with all of the top sites, whether you're a paid advertiser or you're just taking advantage of their free services. This process can be time consuming and not quite as fruitful as other forms of advertising because of the vast amounts of online competition.

What Works?

Take advantage of every free listing service available. Most of the big players in the directory world will let you update your information online. They want a complete directory so more people will come to them for their searches. You only have to pay if you

If you advertise on a search engine, be sure you show up in the first page of search results.

want to do things to put yourself ahead of other advertisers. If you choose to pay for advertisement, it's always a safe bet to see what the competition is doing. Everyone should have a website, but if you're going to pay to get traffic there, it needs to be a good one with lots of pictures, features, and testimonials.

If you choose to advertise on a search engine, try to focus on a specialty of your business when choosing the target words your business will be associated with. If you own a concrete company, the simple word "concrete" is likely to return all kinds of national advertisers, and you may end up buried several pages back. Consider something more specific, such as "stamp pressed concrete" or "decorative concrete." As a general rule of thumb, if you do not show up on the first page of searches, you're wasting your money. Think about your own surfing habits. When you want to buy flowers online, would you keep clicking down to the fifth or sixth page?

SCAM ALERT

Getting your business online opens you to a plethora of online scams. Be leery of any new emails you receive once you're up and running online. Never assume that because someone has a website or a phone number, they are a legit company. Frequently check the web address you are surfing to make sure you're not off on some third-party site. If you're using the ABC website, make sure that's where you remain during your activity. If you click on something that whisks you off to something wild, such as Apha52DTTfox/weregoingtostealyourmoney.com, you need to back out of what you're doing immediately. Although it may cost more to do business with the bigger names out there, it'll get you better results and cut down on your chances of being scammed.

Web Ads

Web ads or banner ads can be one of the most difficult forms of advertising for small businesses to navigate. Built initially to cover large populations, these ads can be refined to give your business some added results if done correctly. Look for localized sites, such as minor league sports teams, local news sites, or any other site whose traffic would generally be limited to local guests.

Pros

Banner ads direct people to your website, which means they are basically glorified and interactive business cards. If you have a great site, it can be extremely valuable to drive buyers to your page, as they can learn about your business without considering your competition.

You often can purchase these ads on a pay-per-click basis, allowing you to pay directly for your results. Just remember to make sure you're dealing with a legitimate business.

Cons

People may have a lower acceptance of online ads than regular "junk mail" because of the scams found online. You may need to already be a well-branded business for people to click through a banner ad in the first place.

Although local sites get a fair amount of usage, their flat-rate pricing tends to be absurdly high. Use your common sense and ask your peers what local sites they check out frequently.

What Works?

No matter how well branded or reputable your company is, there will be no reason for people to click through an ad unless at that exact moment they're thinking about making a buying decision in your industry. Instead of just displaying your name and logo, make an offer to inspire people to click through. "Hughes Auto Dealership Since 1939" might be a recognizable ad, but in order to have a serious click-through rate, "Hughes Auto Dealership: Click to receive free maintenance for a year on your next auto purchase!" would be far more successful.

SCAM ALERT

There's nothing wrong with people starting up new local websites in your area, but don't pay for an ad—no matter how cheap it is—until the site is up and running. A smart webmaster will give away free ads to prove their effectiveness upon the site's creation. Be leery of any medium that is brand new to your area, especially if they want money up front.

Television

Television advertising has long been one of the most powerful yet most expensive advertising mediums available. Watching TV is an American pastime, and even with the introduction of television online and DVRs that can speed through commercials, there are still a lot of opportunities out there to gain customers. Because of these recent changes, television stations and cable companies have done a lot to continue to provide their advertisers with responses. Many local news stations push their own websites that can work in conjunction with a television commercial. This provides you with branding opportunities through traditional commercials and an online presence on a local station–backed website. Cable companies offer numerous sponsorship spots and demographic-specific channels at astoundingly low rates.

Pros

TV commercials are a visual and audio medium for advertising.

Television commercials combine visual and audio aspects that allow you to fully engage your potential customers. You also have a captive audience (if they aren't channel surfing or getting up to fix a snack) who can usually stand to give you 30 seconds of their time. Television is a great way to target both specific demographics and large audiences. A hobby-shop owner can likely find a channel or show on cable that is related to model airplanes or that might be suitable for his or her very specific demographic. A local grocery store could choose to advertise on a local station with the highest-rated five o'clock news in order to reach a wide population.

Television can serve to both brand your business and call your customers to action. A local musical-instrument retailer could run a few ads here and there to help brand the store and then use the same station to run a major ad campaign a few weeks before a huge sale.

Commercials have the advantage of bringing demonstrations right before people's eyes. A before-and-after picture of clean carpets in a print ad can be useful, but a visual of a carpet being cleaned with a voiceover testimonial from a satisfied customer brings your message to life.

Cons

Television commercials are generally very expensive. Local ads can frequently go for hundreds of dollars per spot during peak times and even thousands during top shows and events. Furthermore, these ads need to be run many times to be really effective. Cable ads can work well for companies with specific demographics as clientele, but viewership numbers can be spread extremely thin over the wide range of channels available to the public. You may find cheaper ads on the less viewed programs, but you'll have to run many times more to match the response of an ad during a highly rated show.

It also can be very difficult to track your commercial's success rate. If you're branding your company, it's hard to get the overall picture of how your image is being built. Even when there is a sales event or a call to action, it can be difficult to know who is responding to your spot without having specific conversations with each of your clients.

What Works?

If you are not comfortable with investing thousands of dollars into advertising on television, you're better off staying off the air. Unless you own a business that deals with a very specific demographic that can be targeted with perfection using a cable station or a specific show, you will not get any kind of results from spending a few hundred dollars. If you "try out" television spending very little to test the waters, you'll end up having a bad experience with a medium that can be highly effective.

If you want to try television advertising, be prepared to invest the money to do it well.

The following example depicts a pretty minimal budget of $3,000 to $4,000 per month. More money invested usually gives you more results and better branding, but use your own discretion. Doing much less than the following example will likely result in little or no response. People need to see your message several times for it to catch on and stick with them. Whether you want them to think of you when they need your product or service or you're inviting them to come to a specific sale or event, they need to see your message repeatedly. Using the numbers given to you by sales reps from local stations and your cable provider, figure out which time slots, stations, and programs are favored by your key clientele. Do not be afraid to overlap into stations with mixed demographics if your budget will allow it.

Pick a few of the higher-rated spots and show up with some form of regularity, such as two or three times per week on a solid local news program to get in front of a wide audience. News programs generally have loyal viewers, so you'll get your message across multiple times. What you should *not* do is pick one evening news program across different affiliates and only air your ad once or twice. Most people watch the same channel every night for their local news, so instead of reaching the same people several times per week, you'll reach more people less often. Fifty-thousand people hearing your message three times is far more effective than 150,000 people hearing your message once.

After you pick your prime and more expensive show to run with, find a few more spots where you can run your ad with more frequency, such as a soap opera once a day and/or a game show and/or a national news program, and so on. This will give you a little more frequency with a somewhat smaller audience. Pick a few that are good for your demographic and be sure to be consistent.

Finally, find a few cable stations that fit your demographic. You don't need to pick specific shows, because the numbers will be so small to begin with that it will not be worth nitpicking over. Also, by flooding these stations with ads, you'll end up on the same program multiple times just by pure odds.

Some salespeople will offer to shoot your commercial for free, while others will want to charge a fee. Simply accept the free commercial and use it on other stations. You will usually retain ownership of the spot; just make sure before you sign.

Gimmicky or funny commercials may be memorable, but their messages and attempts at branding on a local level usually are not. How often have you watched a funny national commercial and thought, "Who is this ad for?" before the payoff at the end. National companies spend far more time and money on creating memorable and entertaining commercials because they are expecting you to see the same themed commercial hundreds of times over several months. Locally, you could accomplish this with a large enough campaign, but a few witty commercials will not be enough to brand your business. If you do get sold on a well-written creative commercial, do not be afraid to have your business name or logo left on the screen for the duration of the commercial. If not, you'll be paying for 25 seconds of entertainment and 5 seconds of individual business branding.

Keep your logo, icon, or name on the screen and be sure your business's name is mentioned several times. Every sentence of the script should start with your company's name. It may seem odd on paper or even when you first hear it, but you want to make the most of your spot. If you are creating a spot for an event, keep the branding going but be sure it's clear when your event is and what the big offer is. Mentioning your phone number is important, especially if it's a memorable one, but people will look up your number or simply come to your location anyway.

SCAM ALERT

Although there isn't a lot of malicious activity in the world of television advertising, be sure to keep your best interests in mind. Your rep may push specific inventory because they have too many open slots. Also, don't buy a spot just because it's cheap and you want to get on the air. A commercial at 3:00 a.m. on a station dedicated to rugby may not do a lot for a beauty salon.

Radio

Like television, radio has taken some hits as far as its effectiveness due to recent technological advances. MP3s, satellite radio, and Internet stations have taken some of local radio's listeners, but it is still a good way to generate results. Radio operates in a very similar way to television. Spots are priced based on ratings, and frequency is key.

Frequency is key in radio advertising.

Pros

Radio stations usually enjoy captive audiences. Although people do change the station during some commercials, people usually stick around their favorites. Also, people listening to the radio are usually stuck in one spot, whether they're working, driving, or using the radio as background sound during some kind of task.

Although radio lacks the visual aspect of television, you can use words, sounds, and music to create an image or feeling within the listening audience. People listening to music are more receptive to hearing a jingle or sound-rich commercials when they've been listening to music all along. The same can be said for talk and sports radio. People are paying attention to the voices of their programs, and they stay tuned in for the voices in your spot.

Head to head, radio does not out-pull television, but the cost of an effective radio ad can be much less. You can still target certain demographics, and you can still cover a large population if you run ads on enough stations.

Cons

Radio is just as difficult as television to track. You can ask your customers about your commercials, but again, the branding effect is hard to detect.

In addition, radio stations offer many sponsorship events or remote broadcasts from your location. Sponsoring music festivals or other events can be fun, but the price to brand yourself is usually far more than it's worth. Remote broadcasts rarely draw in the number of people expected, as radio personalities do not have the same popularity as they did before the expansion of television and the creation of the Internet. However, they still sell them because business owners still like the idea of stations broadcasting from their location.

With MP3s and satellite and Internet radio taking a huge portion of the market share, radio stations are not left with as many creative options as television. Most companies are not cutting their rates to reflect reduced listenership, so some spots may end up being overpriced.

Unlike television ads, local radio stations deal directly with national advertising accounts. Because a bulk of their business relies on crunching their numbers with national agencies, local advertisers do not always get the best service from their stations.

What Works?

Similar to television, you do not want to "try out" radio advertising on a shoestring budget. A successful program requires commitment and repetition. The following section provides an example of how a budget of $1,000 to $2,000 per month can have success.

Unlike with television channels, there are far fewer choices when it comes to radio. You can use demographics once again, but focusing on the general population makes more sense. Pick three stations with different programming types. Choosing, say, two country stations is not as effective because they likely share listeners. Consider at least one talk or sports station, a mellow office-friendly station with good numbers, and one or two stations with specific programming to your demographic.

On one of the stations, pick one of the top-rated programs and make sure you have a spot that airs once per day. Make sure the spot is for the specific timeframe for your show. If it's a talk show that runs from noon until three, make sure your spot is for noon until three. If they write it up as noon until six or ten until three, your price will appear lower, but it will likely *not* run during the higher-priced show. Pick one station for the morning commute and a different one for the evening. Once per day for each commute and your top-rated show will pull good numbers, but then you also want to run a high volume of lower-priced spots throughout the day. It's safer to accept ranges for these ads; just make sure midnight to six a.m. is *not* included. It will lower your price, but then you'll have ads running when virtually no one is listening.

Use stories to create an effective radio ad.

Radio stations will usually write and record your commercials for free. Make sure you have different commercials for the different stations based on the listeners. The talk-radio audience will take better to a well-spoken narration about your business, while a pop station will need a little more audio stimulation for its listeners. Radio ads differ from television ads in that you want to tell a story. In television, you want to present your company and give it an image. On the radio, you engage people with "if, then" stories. The "if" hooks the audience, and the "then" tells them what to do.

SCAM ALERT

As with television, there is a lot of accountability in radio advertising, so you're usually pretty safe. Just pay attention to the schedule your sales rep builds for you. If they create wide ranges for your ads to run in order to bring down your price, your spots will likely run in the cheapest time slots available.

Newspaper

Of all the media we've covered, no one has been hit harder than local newspapers. It's easier to find your news online, and most local newspapers have websites to begin with. Online news is free, and you can find a wider range of news on the Internet. Fortunately, some newspapers are learning to become more aggressive with their pricing, and they're offering a wider range of products.

Pros

Being in the newspaper lends credibility to your business.

Many people who still read physical newspapers are very loyal to the publication. There is also still a strong readership in the 50+ age range. Because most of these people have paid subscriptions or buy copies at the newsstand, they welcome the paper into the house along with the included solicitations. Similar to the Yellow Pages, being in the newspaper legitimizes businesses in the eyes of some readers.

Because newspapers are divided into sections, you have the ability to target specific readers within the paper itself. A cigar store advertising in the sports section, makes sense as does a fence contractor being in the home and garden section. Newspapers also have regular data and information, such as sports scores, weather, lotto numbers, and other things that promote repetitive viewing of your ads.

Even though their numbers have slipped, papers still reach a wide audience. Their readers are also all highly engaged—more so than in any other medium. Readers will read articles and be primed to look at your ad. Even people who skim for headlines will still be caught if you have an eye-catching layout.

Cons

Newspapers, similar to radio, are a dying breed, and their rates have not caught up to reality in most cases. If you pick up any paper, most of the ads are national brands and nonprofits, which is a bad sign for local businesses.

Newspapers are starting to produce companion items, such as local magazines, inserts, and websites. Although some of these products are effective and likely help the publisher's bottom line, they end up weakening the paper even further by not trying to improve readership or put out a better base product. If papers don't patch their holes, they'll continue to sink.

The numbers behind newspapers are almost more difficult to follow than television ratings. There are numbers for subscriptions, rack distribution, readership, and so on. The only real way to measure a newspaper ad's effectiveness is to ask around or try it for yourself.

What Works?

Size does not matter as much as frequency when you're advertising in a newspaper. Unless you are a retail store looking to publish prices, you're better off running a sixteenth of a page for a week straight than a full page for one day. Your rep will likely suggest you bounce around to catch the eye of various readers, but I tend to disagree. Most people reading the paper will at least look at every section, even if they only fully read a few. Consistency builds familiarity, and familiarity creates positive branding.

Putting an offer in your advertisement is always a good idea. Most people do not expect to see coupons in the paper, but making special offers for readers is a good way to track your results. "Call and ask about our $299.99 special…" can make your phone ring, and if you keep the offer exclusive to one publication, it will help you know where you're getting your results from.

SCAM ALERT

Although there aren't many fly-by-night newspapers, there may be some small specialized publications that overstate their reach. I once met with an ad rep from a newspaper that was offered free on racks throughout town. She told me they print 25,000 papers, and their readership was 200,000 people per week. So, none of the papers get thrown out? All of them get picked up every week, and then they're each read by eight different people? Use your judgment…

Direct Mail

Direct mail—or "junk mail," as most Americans lovingly call it—is one of the most effective ways to target certain demographics or neighborhoods. Although it is an effective way to solicit people in a one-on-one fashion, it has one of the highest costs per person of any medium. Some companies bring several advertisers together to reduce the postage cost, but I will address those mediums in the next section, "Coupon Publications."

Pros

Direct mail can help you target very specific types of customers.

Most direct-mail companies can help you mail directly to very specific types of customers. If you own a hair-loss clinic, for example, you could select men between the ages of 30 and 60 with an income over $75,000 who own their homes. If that returns too many addresses, you can change the age range to 35 to 55. Once you have an affordable number of addresses, these companies can produce a wide range of products to send to your potential clients. Most companies will offer high-gloss full-sheet mailers with heavy card stock, all the way down to lightweight single-sided postcards.

Some companies can mail entire ZIP codes for your business. If you have a takeout restaurant and don't feel like hand-delivering menus to everyone in your neighborhood, this can be an effective medium.

Although repetition is good for any type of marketing, direct mail is one of the very few forms that can regularly get results with a single impression. An ad in the newspaper for 50-percent off a second suit at a clothing shop might take several impressions before it catches on. However, if someone receives a direct-mail solicitation with the same offer, they'll act on it if they have interest, with just one reception.

Cons

Junk mail is frequently treated as such—hence the name. Your potential buyers are not usually engaged and are often irritated by receiving your mailing. (I hate to jump back to pros now that we've moved on to cons, but I must interject. Every time I hear someone complain about junk mail, I explain to them that it wouldn't exist if it didn't work.)

Also, the price per mailing makes it difficult to reach a large audience. It can often cost thousands of dollars to mail to just 10,000 homes. Direct mail may offer exclusive access to people, but you can't affordably brand yourself or send out a generalized message to the masses.

Direct-mail pieces need a lot of supporting advertising for people to trust your service. You should be in the Yellow Pages, have a website, and do some other branding advertising so that people are comfortable before accepting your mailing.

It can be extremely difficult to find a direct-mail company to do business with. Unlike other mediums, there are not just a few big players that the rest are trying to emulate. It may seem like a pro that there are lots of companies vying for your business, but the reality is that it may be harder to decide who to do business with. Spending such a large amount of money for a one-time transaction can be intimidating, especially if you're not sure who you're dealing with.

What Works?

If your business is already established, direct mail can usually get you some quick and trackable results. First and foremost, make sure your mailing is offer based. Even if you're just mailing a menu for your restaurant, be sure to pack it full of coupons so that people will take action. If you're using direct mail to announce an event, be sure to offer something for the redemption of the mailing piece.

Be sure your direct-mail piece is offer based and gives the customer some incentive to use it.

Select a reasonable mailing area or demographic. If you have a very specific demographic, find a company who can best target it. If keeping things to a ZIP code is what you prefer, be sure that you're getting a good rate for a relatively large mailing.

Find a reputable local company to do the mailing. You could certainly save some money by outsourcing the mailing to a cut-rate company online, but you never really know for sure what you're getting into unless you've talked to many people and read several legitimate reviews. It's also good to find a local company so it's easier to meet with someone for negotiations, ad design, and accountability. Sometimes other advertising mediums offer direct-mail services as well. Try asking your newspaper or Yellow Pages rep whether they have any direct-mail services.

If you want to reach many people, consider breaking up your mailings by week or month to different ZIP codes. You don't want to be stuck with a large immediate bill if it takes you some time to turn your leads into paying customers. Also, it will take you some time to gauge how much of a response you can handle.

SCAM ALERT
As I've mentioned several times in this section, pay close attention to whom you're dealing with. You may find a great deal online, but make sure you use your common sense.

Coupon Publications

Coupon publications are very similar to direct mail except they use multiple advertisers to keep the costs down. I call them coupon publications because coupons are the driving factor behind the medium as a product to consumers. They accept these publications because they are expecting to search for coupons. Usually these publications come in the form of a magazine or a stuffed envelope. Some are mailed directly to homes, while others are distributed through newspapers or on racks throughout your town.

Pros

Coupon publications are a highly cost-effective way to reach a large population.

Because you pay less for postage and production by being represented with other advertisers, coupon publications are one of the most cost-effective ways of reaching large populations. You can often get your message and offer to hundreds of thousands of people for less than $1,000.

People who look through coupon publications are expecting to be solicited and are actively in search of good deals. If you have something they're potentially looking for and the offer is strong enough, you will get calls.

If you use them correctly, coupon publications can brand your business, call consumers to action, and serve as a directory for people to find you. People will see your message on a monthly basis, thus branding your name. Your coupon will call potential buyers to action. Having your business information in the publication on a regular basis will also cause it to serve as a directory, as consumers will be used to seeing your business in the publication.

Cons

With coupon publications, you will lose out on the exclusivity of direct mail while also being subjected to direct competition. If you're a mover with a coupon for $200 off any move, the guy right next to you with $250 off is going to get the first call and likely the consumer's business. If you go up against numerous competitors, the number of active buyers gets divided up even further.

Although there is better usage for coupon publications, they are still frequently considered junk mail. Because of their profitability, more and more options have sprung up, giving you more choices to make and more overload for people receiving these mailings. Also, some mailings will go to apartment dwellers, which some advertisers may not be interested in. (For example, a roofing company won't want to bother marketing itself to apartment renters, who aren't responsible for the exterior of their dwelling.)

Although you're covering a larger population, it's harder to customize your message to different people. Also, the mailings usually come out once per month, giving you a limited shelf life and little time to change your message. You may get dozens of calls a few days after the publication comes out, but your phone isn't going to ring again until the next mailing if you don't have other marketing plans.

You *must* make an offer. A coupon or a clearly stated discount or deal must be present. If you have a very limited margin and very fixed costs, this may not be the place for you.

What Works?

Regardless of the size of advertisement you choose to have published, your offer is the number-one driving factor behind your success with this medium. You must present multiple offers, and they must be bold enough to get people to take action. Think about what you can offer for FREE, buy one get one free, buy one get one half off, an aggressive dollar value off, a large percentage off (15 percent or more)…

Your offer is the driving factor behind your success in advertising in coupon publications.

Most of these publications are high-quality print, so be sure to have a nice picture and keep the text clean and unique. You may be competing with other people in the publication, so make sure to set yourself apart. Although you should always meet with multiple advertising reps, it's especially important to do so when you're advertising in coupon mailers. Most companies can be compared apples to apples because they all usually cover your whole region, which lets you make your decision based on price. The reality is that consumers don't know which coupon magazine or envelope they're looking at; they just know what they're looking for. They don't know who the publisher is or what you're paying for your ad; they're only concerned with your content centered around an offer.

SCAM ALERT

Surprisingly, you need to pay close attention to the pricing of some of the better-known national coupon mailers. They may have good reputations, but there are a lot of smaller local publications that literally mimic the product and its range for a fraction of the cost. In one market, I found three coupon magazines whose circulation was about the same, but the prices for a full page ranged from $3,500 to $1,700 to $650! Just be sure these smaller companies have been around and have provided results for other businesspeople in your area.

Local Magazines

Readers of local magazines are often a captive audience for your ad.

Many communities now have localized magazines available for free or a subscription. Some of these magazines focus on family, homes, age groups, local traffic, and so on. Because you have a captivated reader much like the ones you find for newspapers, you can expect people to spend time looking at your ads.

Pros

Most magazines offer high-quality color printed advertisements that allow you to feature vivid pictures and eye-catching color schemes. Most magazines sell on image as opposed to content, so people are glad to be visually stimulated. If your ad is as interesting as the content, you can get a lot of attention.

Because these magazines are usually for specific demographics, it's easier to target certain people who accept these publications into their homes. You can often talk to the publisher about content and match your ad with articles or even write an article if you're considered a local expert in your field. People's trust levels can vary with any kind of ad, but if you've also contributed some content, consumers will take you even more seriously.

Cons

Because of the high price of publishing magazines, the costs are turned over to you as the paid advertiser. You end up reaching a limited population with considerably higher costs.

It's less popular to make offers in high-end magazines, and in some they're not even allowed. Because of this, it can be difficult to track the results. Without a call to action, your ad is better suited for branding. Unfortunately, you're often branding yourself to a smaller population.

High-end magazines take more time to lay out and produce, so many of your ad decisions have to be made months in advance. If you want to make a change or you find something is not working, several publications may pass before your updated ad is run.

What Works?

Advertising in magazines takes a serious time commitment, which can also come with somewhat of a price tag. You have to be ready to sign on to run your ad for a considerable amount of time, knowing that you may not feel a qualifying response for some time. If you under-spend in radio and television, you will likely get a poor result. If you under-run in a magazine, you will likely face the same kinds of failures. Make sure you select an ad that you can commit to financially for a year and that makes sense for your businesses target demographics. A quarter page will have more success over 12 months than a full page that you may have to cut short because of finances. If the price is right for a full page, by all means go for it. Just be sure to commit yourself for a full year.

As with television and radio, you need to be able to commit fully to a magazine ad campaign to see results from it.

Take the design of your ad very seriously. Although most ads are driven by content, magazine ads need a little more creativity and quite a bit of visual excitement. Copying your bullet point–laden Yellow Pages ad into a magazine will fail.

SCAM ALERT
Pay close attention to circulation numbers and ask your peers what magazines they're familiar with. Although most of these businesses are legitimate, they will do everything they can to dress up their numbers.

Billboards

Billboard campaigns get some of the highest impressions of any form of advertising, yet they are one of the most difficult mediums to track. Because they are usually used exclusively for branding, it's hard to confirm the results. Tens of thousands or even hundreds of thousands of people can see your message every day, so it's important to deliver the most effective message possible.

Pros

Keep your billboard message simple to successfully brand your business.

Tens of thousands of people may see your message every day if you have a high-traffic poster or several lower-traffic posters in a package. By keeping your ad simple, you can brand your business more effectively than you can in any other medium. A giant billboard that simply reads, "Harrison Spas: Your First and Last Stop for All of Your Spa Needs" will drill that concept into people's minds on a daily basis. When people who drive past your billboard think spas, you would certainly be tops for their local list.

Besides branding, billboards can be good devices for announcing events. If people see time and time again that "Father's Day Weekend Is Max's Mattress Sale of the Year," they will in time make that association.

Billboards are great for businesses that want to market to out-of-town visitors. Out-of-towners have nothing better to base their buying decisions on than a well-displayed message they see as they drive through town.

Cons

Billboards can be extremely expensive. High-traffic signs cost into the thousands per month, and the most prime of areas can even top $10,000 in an average city. For smaller signs to be effective, you must purchase several to get the impressions needed for results.

Billboards are very difficult to track. You can make offers, but they have to be pretty limited considering the short amount of time people have to look at your ad. Also, it takes a considerable amount of time for your message to be absorbed by commuters. You may have to spend a serious amount of money for several months before you even notice an increase in business.

People only have a few seconds to read most billboards, so your messages have to be limited. If you have dozens of services or products to offer, you must focus on one, or else your message will be lost.

Billboards are not priced by actual cost; rather, they're priced by daily impressions. Someone actually takes the time to monitor how many vehicles pass by a particular location over the course of an average day. Production costs are the same: A billboard that has 500,000 views per month costs the same to produce as a billboard that gets 20,000 views per month (give or take based on the land value). Thus, price is determined by daily impression.

The price to maintain billboards and pay for the property pales in comparison to what billboard companies earn per sign. This may not seem like a negative in a capitalist society, but it is important to know you are paying for assessed value, not nuts and bolts. You'll find a lot of national brands and nonprofits buying billboards because it's an easy way for them to spend their advertising money and get a lot of impressions with minimal maintenance.

What Works?

Similar to magazines, you must commit to a considerable amount of time to ensure results with billboards. Three or four months, minimum, is what you must consider if you want to get a return on your investment. If you have a regional business that serves a large area, consider going for one of the highest-traffic billboards available or several smaller street-level billboards in the specific neighborhoods that you find many of your customers.

> Be prepared to invest at least three or four months into your billboard advertising campaign.

Make sure your message is extremely brief and not confusing. A bold picture is fine, but make sure your name and your single branding idea are featured. There is no need to include your phone number unless it's part of your name or extremely brandable (such as 555-555-5555—you get the idea).

Your billboard rep will tell you to move your billboard around monthly. Do not agree to do this under any circumstances. This is an extremely self-serving program for these companies to undertake. They need signs to turn over so that no one is getting free advertising. If everyone stayed in the same spot but one guy stopped paying, his message would stay up there until they bring in a new advertiser. The idea of rotating your ad only serves to prevent this. You want your ad to stay in the same place so that your message is drilled into consumers' minds and never leaves them. They need to see your billboard in the same place over and over so they assume that you are the sole owner of that sign. Also, taking down a sign for a business always triggers negative thoughts from the consumer. "Did they move? Go out of business? Is business bad?"

SCAM ALERT

Make sure you physically inspect each sign location to know what you're getting into, especially if you purchase multiple street-level locations. I had a sales rep tell me that one of my street-level signs would be facing oncoming commuter traffic to the downtown area. When the sign went up, I went to look after the fact and realized that it was facing a condemned apartment building on a street no one uses. He sold me another sign that he claimed had higher viewership than it was priced at because of a detour. It turned out the detour prevented people from even driving by the sign.

Signage and In-Store Marketing

If you have a retail storefront or even an office for people to visit, you have a great chance to market to already engaged buyers. They can learn about other products or services without even having a conversation with you. Outdoor signage takes advantage of natural pedestrian and commuter traffic and is similar to having your own billboard without paying a premium. You should also use vehicles and jobsites to brand and deliver your message.

Pros

You have to have a location, vehicles, jobsites, and storefronts any-way, so you might as well take advantage of these opportunities for very little added cost. Most areas have many sign companies, so you can get very competitive pricing for printing on or wrap-ping your vehicles, hanging a banner or fixed signs, and placing jobsite signs.

Having an outdoor sign on your store-front or office is like having your own billboard, but without the high cost.

Once you've paid the initial cost of setting up these marketing pieces, there is no cost to keep them going other than minor maintenance.

Further, high visibility of your company's day-to-day activity can create a good sense of security for your potential clients. They will be far more likely to call you than someone who they have never seen out in the community.

Retailers can use simple signage to move sale items, clear out inventory, or feature new products to consumers with whom they are already doing business.

Cons

Although signage and in-store marketing do brand your business, they don't usually do enough to bring in new customers. A grand-opening sign on a pizza shop is great, but a coupon in the mail is even better.

Further, some signage and car wrapping can get expensive if you let yourself get carried away. If your budget is limited, your money is better spent elsewhere.

What Works?

Make sure your storefront or office is easy to find. At least get some magnets for your car or other vehicles with your name and contact info. If you do work off site, be sure to have signs clearly posted so people can experience your work firsthand. Keep any in-store signage neat and easy to read.

Social Networking: Online and Real Life

Networking, whether in person or online, is a vital part of promoting your business.

Social networking has always been an important part of marketing businesses, but recently online social sites have proven to be useful in amplifying people's messages. Social events are a great way to make a name for yourself, regardless of what business you're in. And staying in touch with your new contacts is now even easier with these social websites.

Pros

When you've gained enough friends or followers, you can convey messages to them and their contacts for free. A great real estate agent I know uses her social-media accounts for personal updates but announces new listings to her warm audience of friends and acquaintances. They may be interested in the property themselves, or they may pass the info on to a friend who's in the market for a new home.

Social events are great if you have an agreeable personality. People quite simply prefer doing business with people they like or can at least tolerate. Just as with online socializing, the person you meet at a business mixer may not need any help with estate planning, but maybe his mother-in-law has been looking for a good referral. You never know what kinds of customer you might uncover through friendly conversations.

Besides, social events are fun! You likely got into business for yourself because you want to get the most out of life, so don't forget to enjoy yourself!

Cons

It can take some time to build up a social network that will provide enough leads to keep you in business. Handing out business cards at a fundraiser is a good idea, but a direct-mail piece will get you more results much faster.

Events can be expensive. Workshops, seminars, fundraisers, and mixers can be quite costly, especially if you only add one or two social contacts to your list.

And don't forget that social-networking messages can become invasive and annoying if you overdo it. People are on these sites for social reasons and can tolerate a few messages here and there, but if you message everyone twice a day about your vitamin inventory, you'll probably lose friends quickly.

Don't be obnoxious with your social-networking attempts at promoting your business.

What Works?

Use social-networking sites and events to socialize. They take a long time to increase your customer base, so do not count on them as a sole source of business. Pass out business cards wherever you go and message your friends online—just don't be obnoxious.

Other Mediums

Besides these mainstream mediums, there are many other unique places you can consider advertising. Some get good results; some may be a bit laughable. If there's a blank space and people are looking, there'll be advertising there soon.

Church Bulletins

People have a strong affinity for their church and its bulletin, so it's a great publication in which to place an ad if they allow it. Some churches outsource the sale of ad space, so you may have to pay a bit more in premiums to be listed. Use common sense. Several-hundred people may see your message in a publication that is important to them; just make sure it's priced right. It'll be several times more effective if you are a parishioner.

Movie Theaters

If you ever show up early to your local movie theater, you'll either see a slideshow of ads or some short commercials before the coming attractions. From what I've seen, these ads can be absurdly expensive, so make sure you get the most out of your ad if you decide to run one. Be sure you make an offer that is valid with the ticket stub to help you track your results. And remember to pay attention to the demographics of your local theaters before you decide to advertise. Although most people go to the movies at some point, there are certainly demographics that will show up more frequently.

Donations and Sponsorships

Of course you want to give back to the community, but there's nothing wrong with getting a little credit for your act of benevolence. Sponsoring your child's baseball team? Don't forget to hang your banner and keep some pictures of the team in your office! Donating to a local charity? Let them mention it in their newsletter. Better yet, mention you are a proud sponsor of ABC Charities in your next advertisement! It's okay if everyone wins when you give back to the community. Besides being tax deductible, it's a great way to show the community that you're not a cold-hearted businessperson.

Local Sports Teams

Most areas have some college, semi-pro, minor league, or pro teams in their town. Branding yourself with a team that people in your community follow can give your business a bit of a boost. Some sponsorship can be cost prohibitive, though. Be sure to have your basic advertising program in place before you make any decisions to advertise with a team. They can capitalize on the fact that you're a fan, so the pricing tends to be a little overboard. On the flip side, advertising with teams can lead to some fun perks you may enjoy if you're a fan.

Flyers

Flyers are basically direct-mail pieces without the postage. They can come across as juvenile or invasive, though, as you are not legally supposed to put anything in anyone's mailbox. Consider flyers when you're working in an area so you can introduce people in the neighborhood to your work. If you're opening up a new storefront, grand-opening flyers delivered by you, the business owner, may be a good way for you to get to know your neighbors. Do *not* put them in people's mailboxes. Consider using door-jambs, welcome mats, and so on instead. Just remember to keep them to a minimum and try not to be too invasive.

Promotional Items

It might be fun to see your name on mugs, pens, T-shirts, and notepads, but it will likely do little for your business. It may keep you on the minds of your repeat customers if you gift these items, but don't expect a huge return on this investment. Most people selling these things are doing so by tapping into your ego. Feel free to have a few fun things around the office with your name on them; just don't get carried away.

Receipts

Yes, you can advertise on the backs of receipts in many big retail and grocery stores. However, the one time I priced out this product, it made no sense for my business. But if you're a retailer in the same plaza as the store offering the ad space, you may find some value in these receipt ads. Just don't forget to include an offer!

Urinals

If you think customers relieving themselves in front of your logo may be profitable for your business, have at it....

With any advertising medium, whether mainstream or unusual, use your common sense. Does the pricing reflect your anticipated results? Will this move help you retain your current customer base while bringing in new clients? It's important to take an objective look at all advertising mediums before building your complete marketing strategy.

Action Plan

To create an effective marketing plan or improve upon your existing strategies, you need to familiarize yourself with your local advertising mediums. Answering these questions will lay the groundwork for the next chapter, which covers implementing your marketing strategy.

✓ How many local Yellow Pages are available, and which ones are people using?

✓ Have you built a website, and if so, will it be worth driving online traffic to it?

✓ What radio and television stations seem to be the most popular and have the most local commercials airing?

✓ What local companies offer direct mail or coupon publications?

✓ How strong are your local newspapers?

✓ What billboards in your area have the most impact on you as a consumer, in terms of both location and message?

✓ What condition or stage are your storefront/signage/fleet in?

✓ How well connected are you socially, both online and in the flesh, and what events might you consider attending for networking purposes?

✓ What other forms of advertising are out there in your community?

Chapter 5

Implementing a Marketing Strategy

- Advertising Budget
- Directional, Creative, and Call-to-Action Advertising
- Case Studies
- Action Plan

Now that you're more familiar with your business, customers, and different advertising mediums, you need to come up with a marketing strategy. No two businesses, customer bases, markets, or mediums are completely alike, so there is no set template for creating a marketing strategy. Senior citizens in Southern California likely make their buying decisions differently than senior citizens in Michigan. A newspaper in Baltimore may reach a completely different audience than a newspaper just an hour south in Washington, D.C. An orthodontist in Oklahoma may need a completely different strategy than one in North Carolina does. By knowing your customers, your business, and the advertising mediums available to you, as well as using a bit of common sense, you can accomplish any of your business goals.

It may seem like a backwards process to build a marketing strategy without first meeting with your advertising sales reps. However, it's important for you to figure out what you want before you are "sold" on anything else. Your sales reps are an extremely useful resource for comparing market information and giving you a perspective on their product versus others in the area. But as honest and helpful as they might be, they will always be selling you on their product or service. By building a strategy first, you avoid making any decisions based on pressure or even a good pitch. Otherwise, you might like what the billboard guy has to say and spend several thousand dollars, only to find that radio may have been a better decision. Or, you may end up under-committing to a bunch of mediums without even being sure what your plan is.

Advertising Budget

Your advertising budget is the most important part of your marketing strategy and is completely impossible to define. Doesn't make sense? It doesn't, and it really shouldn't....

It's impossible to define your advertising budget. If you set a certain amount toward advertising, you'll find yourself making decisions based on that number.

If you sit down at the beginning of your fiscal year and say, "We're going to spend $30,000 on marketing this year," you're going to make decisions based solely on dollar value. This is a problem I have seen with many nonprofit companies. They operate on a fixed budget because what they do is not about generating revenue. They take that $30,000, buy a few low-rated spots on radio and television, and then call it a day. Nonprofits could have more success if they spent their advertising budget like a for-profit company, but I digress....

You are in business to make money. Every sales rep you sit down with will tell you the same story when they're trying to convince you to advertise. "If you give me a $1 bill, and I give you a $5 bill, would you take that deal? Of course you would—you'd take it all day." They're right, but only to an extent.

If a taxidermist spent $1,000,000 on television ads in his town, would he make $5,000,000? Absolutely not. If he spent $10,000 on television ads in his town, focusing on hunting and pet shows, is it possible he may see a profit? Yes.

If a law firm spent $1,000,000 on television ads in their town, would they make $5,000,000? Possibly! If a law firm spent $10,000 on television ads in their town, would they see a profit from that investment? Probably not. More than likely, they would be drowned out by all of the other advertisers with more aggressive campaigns.

You can see how there is no real way to define an effective advertising program based solely on dollars spent. When you invest in the stock market as an individual, you research particular stocks and trends; you look at the market as a whole and bump it against your goals as an individual. The same can be said about advertising. You have to consider everything we've discussed in earlier chapters. What are your business goals? Where are your primary customers? What are your competitors doing? What is the market doing? Which mediums mesh best with your needs? No set dollar value can guarantee anything (unless you spend $0—that guarantees you will not get any new non-referral business).

How about Dave the plumber, who works by himself? The $1,000,000 on television is a no-go, and likely the $10,000 dollars on TV is a bad idea as well. What if Dave took that $10,000 and invested it into the Yellow Pages with a half-page ad reading, "24 HOUR EMERGENCY SERVICES!"? That's perfect; now he can get those calls where he can charge a little more by being available immediately.

With this advertising strategy, business is great for Dave the plumber over the next year! In fact, he's decided to hire a receptionist and three more plumbers so he can take on more work. His Yellow Pages sales rep gets a shock when Dave wants a huge two-page ad and the outside back cover of the book, still touting the 24-hour emergency services, *plus* he features a one-hour water-heater replacement service. His Yellow Pages bill jumps to $36,000, but he declares, "This is all I'm spending for the rest of the year on advertising."

Several months later, the book comes out, Dave's calls increase, and all is well. A sales rep from a direct-mail company sees the ad and decides to make a sales visit. Dave is presented with an offer to have all homeowners in his area with homes valued over $100,000 direct-mailed a sticker that they can place on their water heater so they will be likely to call him when they need the water heater replaced. It's only $2,000 per month to cover the whole city over the course of a year. Another $24,000 for the year—what should Dave do? Does he increase his advertising budget, or does he stick to his original number and pass up the potential for more business?

Advertising investments are like any others: There are no guarantees.

Of course, these are extreme examples, but you can see how much of the decision-making has less to do with dollar value and more to do with your business and a variety of circumstances. With Dave's story, we're headed to return on investment. You probably have already heard of this, and if you've ever sat down with an advertising sales rep, you've watched them do their fuzzy math and show you how you can't lose by advertising with them. Again, they're correct to an extent, but you have to paint a larger picture to make your decision. There's a limit to the amount of business a taxidermist can conduct in most towns. The law practice that decided to go with only $10,000 for the year is likely not going to see much of a return on investment because they under-committed in a flooded medium. What the sales reps don't tell you is that these investments are like any other: There's no guarantee.

Dave the plumber might debate the idea of the direct-mail campaign. He charges $2,000 for same-day, one-hour emergency water heater replacement, so his sales rep tells him he only needs one call per month to break even. But we all know that's not the case. First of all, Dave only converts one out of four calls into sales. Second, the unit costs Dave $1,000, and the labor is $200. So now Dave is looking at making $800 every four calls, and that's only considering immediate costs. To simply break even, Dave needs 120 calls to get 30 jobs that year. For math reasons, let's say that his $24,000 campaign delivers to 48,000 homes. Dave assumes water heaters need to be replaced every 10 years, meaning 4,800 homes will need service each year. If only one in ten households takes his sticker and calls him when they're in need, he should get 480 calls for the year. That's 360 more calls than he needs, equaling $72,000 in profit.

These numbers all sound good because they can be backed up by simple math. The only problem is that there's no way to know whether Dave is going to get one out of ten homeowners to use his sticker. If only one in 100 uses his sticker, that's only 48 calls! The only way Dave could ensure high usage is if he takes time to build an effective message. We'll cover effective messages in Chapter 7, "Content and Offers," but let's take on Dave's case right now.

If Dave sends out the sticker with just his name and phone number on it, he's probably not going to see a return on his investment. A more effective sticker might have a border with the words "Please peel and stick to your water heater," repeated around the outside, for example. In bold, large print set against a bright red or yellow background, the sticker should read, "For 24-hour IMMEDIATE service or replacement of this water heater, please call Dave's Plumbing at 555-555-5555." And perhaps a small warning: "Danger: Do not attempt to repair this unit on your own!" Basically, he needs to include something that would give the sticker more value while encouraging people to put it up.

As you can see, an advertising budget is hard to define. If Dave decided to spend $10,000 on television in the first place, who knows what might have happened? If he didn't take a chance and up his Yellow Pages investment, he never could have hired the new employees. Should Dave spend more to send out these stickers? If he sticks to his word and spends no more money on advertising, his answer will be no. If he decides to do the mailing, maybe he'll come up short. Then again, maybe he'll add six figures of profit to his bottom line and be able to hire a full-time water heater specialist. (As a side note, I'd advise him to take the deal. If the mailing company is reputable and it's a stand-alone piece, 50 cents per house isn't bad for a sticker, and the reality is that he'll be getting a return on that particular investment for years to come. He should order some overrun on the stickers so he can put them on new water heaters himself!)

The other problem with establishing a set budget is that it will show up on your balance sheet as a cost. If times become tough, and you feel the need to make cuts within your business, advertising too often is one of the first things to go. Unfortunately, hastily cutting your advertising can cause your business to miss out on potential income and fall further into hard times. Word of mouth can get you a lot of business, but you still need to present yourself to the public, even when times are tough.

Directional, Creative, and Call-to-Action Advertising

The three types of advertising are directional, creative, and call-to-action.

When you first sit down to create your marketing strategy, it is important to consider the three types of advertising that exist. Each of these three categories borrows from the others, but for the most part, they play a set role. No matter the size of your program, you will need a healthy mix of all three.

Directional Advertising

When people already know who or what they need, they turn to forms of directional advertising. Directional advertising "directs" consumers to the exact business or industry they were looking for. A buyer who needs a refrigerator repaired immediately will likely pick up the phone book to be directed to refrigerator repairmen. Maybe that same buyer knows Doug's Refrigerator Repair and just looks up his number online.

Directional advertising mediums include the Yellow Pages, online directories, search engines, and so on—anywhere people might go to get a phone number when they're ready to make a buying decision. It's extremely important that you make sure to at least be listed in all of these places. If you're a kennel that spent thousands of dollars on a beautiful television ad, but your number isn't listed in the phone book under kennels, consumers will just call your competition. If you're lucky, they may turn to the Internet when they don't find you in the phone book, so you need to be easy to find online as well.

You may choose to pay for advertising in these places because people do not always have someone in mind when they start looking. If someone needs his driveway sealed, he may look under "driveways" in the Yellow Pages or online. If he sees 20 listings but only three ads, he'll likely call one of the advertisers. Between the advertisers, he'll first call whoever seems to best fit what he's looking for. Maybe he'll call the driveway guy boasting the lowest rates in town. Maybe he'd rather go with the company ensuring a quick turnaround. Either way, the advertisers will get the most attention if the person doesn't already have a specific business in mind.

You need to be listed in many places to make sure potential customers can find you.

Online searches may be a little different. Businesses must pay premiums to be listed first or at the top of various search engines and directories. Showing up early in online lists usually leads to more calls. That same person looking for a fresh top-coat on his driveway may simply get estimates from the first three listings that come up on his favorite online directory. Or, he may choose to do business with one of the earlier listings that has a link to its professional website.

As you can see, you must be listed in many places to make sure your potential customers can find you, and you'll need to advertise in order to sway the uncertain buyers.

Creative Advertising

Creative advertising is any form of advertising that can be used to brand your business. Billboards, radio and television commercials, sponsorships, signs, bumper stickers, and so on—anywhere you can get your name out to create an image for your company and a familiar feeling for the consumers. If Bill owns a boat shop, he could have a billboard that simply says, "BILL'S FOR BOATS" with a picture of a beautiful speedboat. He may buy a 10-second spot on the radio to sponsor the half-hour news: "This news segment was brought to you by Bill's Boats. Go to Bill's for boats!" To top it off, Bill may have every bus-stop bench plastered with the words, "BILL'S FOR BOATS!" This example is a little simplified and over the top, but it shows you basically what branding does. Anyone living in that town for a few months would know where they could shop for boats.

Creative advertising brands your business.

Creative advertising can be a very powerful method to build your business over the long run. If Bill ran a coupon in a coupon magazine offering a free trailer with the purchase of any new boat, he'd probably get a response of some sort every time the magazine was delivered. However, if that was the only advertising Bill did, he would likely be idle until the next edition came out. Without creative advertising to brand his company, people would not automatically associate him with boats.

If Bill started an effective television campaign displaying his wide array of boats, financing available, and so on, people would start to associate him with boats and consider seeing him before any of his competition. The coupons would give a nice boost here and there, but the branding he's done would build his business's momentum. He might not get the immediate results the coupons would give him, but the public's awareness of his boat lot would continue to grow.

It's not as easy to give a rule of thumb with creative advertising. With directional, you must have at least the minimum to succeed. Creative can go either way. Very small businesses can often get by on just on referrals and a properly listed phone number. However, without creative advertising, the only people who will know about your service are the ones who have already done business with you or who've been referred by others. And if you have a business in which you're not seeing your customers on a monthly or better basis, they may forget to refer you to others, or someone else's advertising may sway them. If you use creative advertising, you can strengthen those referrals, because you do not need to resell yourself to your existing customers. They'll see your name from time to time, and it will keep you fresh in their memory.

Think of that picture you have of an old friend you haven't seen in a while. You get a comforting feeling without someone having to tell you why you guys were friends in the first place. Let's say you look at that picture, and the next day your spouse tells you he or she is throwing you a birthday party, and you should invite all of your friends. Maybe you'll think about contacting that old friend because you just saw his picture recently. If you hadn't seen that picture, you might not have thought to send the invite. It doesn't mean that person is a bad friend; he was just someone who you hadn't thought about in a while.

Creative advertising operates on similar premises. Besides branding your name to people who have never dealt with you, you strengthen your existing bonds. Let's say you had a great experience with Carl's Carpets, who installed your carpets three years ago. While you're outside, your neighbor is making small talk and mentioning work she's having done, as well as waiting on some estimates from some carpet installers. If the last time you thought about Carl was when you handed over the check three years ago, you'd probably wish your neighbor luck and go on with your day. However, if you drive by Carl's billboard every day on the way to work, you've thought about him, consciously or subconsciously, virtually every day! Now when you hear your neighbor's story, you'll probably say, "Make sure you get an estimate from Carl's Carpets. He did a great job on our house, and his prices were reasonable." Who knows? Maybe your neighbor saw the billboard too and already gave him a call.

In my opinion, creative advertising is best for businesses that have been around long enough to have an existing customer base or for startup companies that have a healthy amount of startup capital. A well-funded startup can hit the ground running if they have the money to heavily brand from the get-go. However, if you've just started a business and have limited money to work with, you may end up going too small with your branding and not generating enough initial business to keep going. An ad that plays once a week on the radio and a single banner on the outfield wall of a local college baseball stadium probably won't cut it. A new business with limited startup capital is better off investing in their directional advertising and call-to-action advertising.

Call-to-Action Advertising

Call-to-action (CTA) advertising is any kind of advertising that encourages the consumer to make an immediate buying decision. Although any kind of advertising can cross over as a form of CTA advertising, the traditional mediums include direct mail, coupon publications, web ads, newspaper, and in-store ads—anything where the messages usually direct people to make a buying decision. These are some of the best mediums for getting immediate but temporary results. If a woman looking at a coupon magazine

Call-to-action advertising encourages consumers to make immediate buying decisions.

finds a coupon (with an expiration date) from a salon for a free manicure with any pedicure for new clients, she'll likely act on it if she doesn't have an exclusive provider for her beauty services. If a homeowner gets a direct-mail coupon for $600 off any new roof, and he has been thinking about getting an estimate, that roofer will likely get a call. The roof was a thought in the homeowner's mind, but the coupon will inspire him to make a call. A newspaper ad might have a clearance sale announced for a local electronics store. Anyone who sees that ad and has a need for electronics (or even a curiosity about the sale) will consider coming to the sale.

CTA advertising is great for seasonal businesses that want to catch their customers when they're contemplating purchases. Contractors can fill up their schedule with strong offers early in the season. Retail stores can take advantage of CTA ads any time of year for sales, but they always come out in heavy numbers around various holidays.

Newer businesses can benefit the most from call-to-action advertising. Companies need to generate sales early and often in order to stay in business. While they spend time branding their image, it's important to grow their existing customer list. Referrals and creative advertising will allow for some steady growth, but aggressive offers in these mediums will help them grow exponentially. Every customer who comes in responding to a coupon or a sales announcement has the potential to be a repeat customer for life. If these customers are satisfied, they, too, will give you referrals.

Let's imagine that for every four satisfied customers Chris's Lawn-Mowing Service gets, they gain a new customer. That may be an aggressive number, but CTA ads will still prove useful. In their first month, they work on a friend's lawn, and they also do three of their relatives' properties. That's four in the first month. With the four-for-one referral system, they'll have five customers the next month, then six, then seven, and then at eight, they start getting two referrals per month. Take a look at Table 5.1.

Table 5.1 Chris's Lawn-Mowing Service

Month	Existing Customers	Referrals	Next Month's Customers
January	4	1	5
February	5	1	6
March	6	1	7
April	7	1	8
May	8	2	10
June	10	2	12
July	12	3	15
August	15	3	18
September	18	4	22
October	22	5	27
November	27	6	33
December	33	8	41

As you can see in Table 5.1, by the end of the year Chris will have a healthy customer base of 41. We'll assume attrition would keep the customer base leveled out around 41 for years to come. Chris could mow two lawns a day by himself for the rest of his life and be content because his wife followed the next example!

Chris's wife, Mary, owns a pool-cleaning service. Coincidentally, she starts with the same four customers with the same four-for-one referral rate. However, she decides to run a coupon in a coupon magazine that goes to most of the homes in the area. She gets a reasonable addition of four customers per month from her ad. Take a look at her numbers in Table 5.2.

Table 5.2 Mary's Pool-Cleaning Service

Month	Existing Customers	Referrals	Coupon Response	Next Month's Customers
January	4	1	4	9
February	9	2	4	15
March	15	3	4	22
April	22	5	4	31
May	31	8	4	43
June	43	10	4	57
July	57	14	4	75
August	75	18	4	97
September	97	24	4	125
October	125	31	4	160
November	160	40	4	204
December	204	51	4	259

As you can see, Mary grew her customer base to 259 people, thanks to her coupon ad. By July she hired an assistant, and by the end of the year she needed to hire another employee. Seeing her success, the next year Chris followed Mary's marketing advice, and they lived happily ever after....

These numbers could hold true for any kind of advertising in general, but the immediate and trackable response is what makes call-to-action advertising so effective. In the years to come, Chris and Mary could ease up on the call-to-action advertising and consider more creative advertising. They may rekindle some of their old customer base and amplify the results of their ads in the coupon publication.

If I have to explain to you that coupons and call-to-action advertising work for retail shops and restaurants, you've probably been living under a rock for a few decades. Pizza shops, takeout restaurants, and even some high-end restaurants use coupons to keep people coming back and to introduce new customers to their food. Retailers live by the sale. All kinds of events and offers keep their doors swinging.

Specialty businesses also seem to have a lot of success with CTA ads, because they often have to inspire their potential customer base to take action. Most people don't wake up in the morning and decide that they have to have a decorative concrete patio poured. However, if they're exposed to a beautiful ad showing what can be done with decorative concrete, along with a firm offer for a free gift with any estimate, they're likely to take it into consideration. Most people like to travel, but they might never have thought to book an Alaskan cruise until they saw an ad for a local travel agency in the newspaper.

Some business owners sneer at the idea of call-to-action advertising. They feel it cheapens their image and turns off big-ticket spenders. I can tell you from experience that I've seen just as many doors close on self-proclaimed "high-end" stores as I've seen on 80-year-old businesses still offering coupons and sales on their products or services. Even people with expendable money like to find a bargain. Your service may be hundreds or even thousands more than your competitor, but if customers were brought in on an offer, they still may do business with you. Whether your business is based on high-end quality or low rates and volume, consumers always like to see offers.

Mixed Forms

Although all forms of advertising fall into one of these categories, most share traits with each other. You could have a directive Yellow Pages ad that also has a call-to-action message inside the book. You may also buy the spine of that book, allowing you to put your business name across the binding so as to brand your company every time someone looks up a number. Radio and television are creative forms of branding advertising, but they frequently contain a call-to-action message. You can use these mediums to announce sale events or one-time offers that will cause people to act quickly. Although newspapers are usually intended to advertise sales, they also indirectly act as a branding medium, as people will see your offer on a more frequent basis. Even billboards can cross over if the message is right. Our old buddy Bill could change his billboard one month to read, "BILL'S FOR BOATS! 0% financing for the month of May!" An ad for an interior designer in a high-end magazine could offer a free gift with any consultation. Lose the dash marks that normal coupons use to encourage consumers to cut them out, and you will keep the image high end while still making an offer.

Most forms of advertising share traits with the other forms of advertising as well. A directive ad may contain a call to action, for example.

The more you can combine these three forms of advertising, the more effective your marketing campaign will be overall. A solid directional presence, aggressive offers and sales, and consistent creative branding can help any business flourish.

Case Studies

I have created six examples of varying companies with different business goals. I'll explain each of their circumstances and provide a marketing solution. Again, there is no formula for what will work in *every* business situation due to so many variables being present. After everything you learn here, common sense should always have the final say. Some of these examples may be similar to your business, and some may be completely different, but you can learn from various parts of all of these strategies.

Case Study 1

Name: Claire's Flower Shop

Business Type: Retail flower shop

Years in Business: 0

Gross Revenue: 0

Employees: 2

Circumstances

Claire was working as an accountant for six years when she was suddenly laid off. Tired of the office world, she has decided to open a flower shop. Her father owns a landscaping-supply company, so she has a fair amount of experience with flowers and some basic knowledge of running a business. Her shop is being set up, and she plans to open the doors in six weeks. She'd like to get a good amount of retail walk-in sales, but her goal is to provide floral arrangements for weddings in her area.

Marketing Solution

The first thing Claire needs to do is contact the sales offices of the two big Yellow Pages in her town. Yellow Pages have a one-year sales cycle, so she needs to make sure her number is listed in the next editions. Upon meeting with her sales reps, she finds that the florist heading is already heavily saturated. Claire purchases an in-column text ad in both books that focuses on floral arrangements for events. One of the Yellow Pages has a wedding guide, so she duplicates her ad in that section. Claire also goes online to make sure all of the major directories and search engines have her contact information.

To drive her retail sales, Claire gets in touch with a sales rep from a local coupon magazine. She decides to go with an aggressive ad to coincide with her grand opening. One coupon is for a free wildflower or three-rose bouquet. She limits the coupon by making it only valid May 1, 2, and 3, the first days of her grand opening. Also included is a coupon for a free vase with any purchase of a dozen roses and a coupon for $5 off any purchase over $20.

Claire meets with her local newspaper rep and places an ad in the wedding and engagement announcements offering free consultations for wedding-flower arrangements. It's run once per week along with the announcements, keeping the costs low but the targeted audience very distinct.

Claire takes out a small ad with three of the nearby churches, mentioning her retail shop and flower arrangements for weddings, funerals, and other church events.

Because her storefront is in a high-traffic area, she invests in a beautiful storefront sign as well as banners announcing the grand opening and her special offers for the event.

Claire used her marketing strategy to introduce her store to the general public while seeking out her primary customers. Later on, she should consider some high-end magazines with beautiful photos of her arrangements, and she should also be sure to have a good website with plenty of pictures to ensure continued success.

Case Study 2

Name: Pete's Painting

Business Type: General painting contractors

Years in Business: 2

Gross Revenue: $175,000

Employees: 4

Circumstances

Pete has had good amount of success in his first two years. His prices aren't the lowest, but he gets good referrals from his high-quality work. He runs his own crew and works with his men, but he wants to be able to expand and concentrate on sales instead of doing the work himself. If he can get the business to support it, he'd like to have three or four crews, each with its own foreman.

Marketing Solution

Pete already has his listings set up, and he's also gotten some business using a small classified ad. His company is set up to meet all kinds of painting needs, so the first thing he does is invest in a display ad in his local Yellow Pages. A quarter-page spot gives him the third largest ad in the heading and allows him to list all of their specialties and display a photo of a completed house.

In the past, Pete has had the best experience with older homeowners. They're willing to pay a little more for a professional job because most have learned from experience. He decides to direct-mail all homeowners in his area who are over the age of 65. He builds the ad to feature a senior discount of $300 off any full exterior or interior paint job.

Because his company can cater to all kinds of painting needs, Pete runs a television commercial during the evening news showing the start-to-finish completion of a home. He also runs some commercials on cable stations that have high viewership by business owners, featuring his commercial and industrial painting services.

Pete receives an immediate response from his senior mailing, allowing him to add more employees. As the residential jobs are completed, he begins to get more calls for commercial and industrial estimates. After the coupon response tapers off, the new Yellow Pages hit the streets, and his call levels begin to increase. Later on, Pete decides to advertise in some local business magazines and runs a few generalized offers in a local coupon-envelope mailing.

Pete needed an immediate response to grow his company and then some active branding to build his business's reputation. He's now a familiar name and has achieved top-of-mind status when residents and business owners think about painting.

Case Study 3

Name: Daryl's Dry Cleaning

Business Type: Storefront drycleaners

Years in Business: 12

Gross Revenue: $300,000

Employees: 6

Circumstances

Daryl has been in business for some time now. He has some small in-column ads in the Yellow Pages and has a selection of coupons go out each month. Business has seemed to hit a plateau and even taper off a bit over the past few years. If he doesn't start to rebuild his customer list, he may not make it much longer.

Marketing Solution

Daryl needs to bring in new customers and possibly expand his services to stay competitive. The local newspaper has a website that has very good usage. Considering that most people getting their local news online are local office people, he purchases a banner ad offering a buy-one-get-one-free dry cleaning service for new clients.

Daryl has always done regular laundry services as well, but it has not been a very popular service. He decides to take out an ad in the college newspaper featuring one-day laundry service at an aggressive price.

Not every business problem has to be smashed with an expensive marketing program. Daryl made some simple but creative additions to his marketing program to keep his employees busy and his bottom line growing!

Case Study 4

Name: Ray's Rare Reptiles

Business Type: Unique and unusual pets

Years in Business: 2

Gross Revenue: $40,000

Employees: 0

Circumstances

Ray has been selling exotic pets on the side for a couple of years. Most of his customers have been friends and acquaintances or leads from his website. Ray wants just a little more business so he can quit his job at Daryl's Dry Cleaning and be fully self-employed.

Marketing Solution

Ray is dealing with a very limited population, so they may be more difficult for him to target. He decides to run a few ads on a cable station that features shows about animals. The channel is not highly rated or expensive, but the audience is very targeted.

Ray is also a pretty popular guy in town. He uses his well-built online social-networking profile to direct people to his business's profile and website. With all the warm leads, Ray starts getting more hits.

Finally, he decides to sponsor a few local Little League teams. The cost was reasonable, and kids are some of his top customers.

After his newfound success, Ray leaves the dry cleaning company. When his sales go up, he decides to spend some money on search engines so that he can serve customers outside his town who are willing to travel a bit for his unique pet offerings.

Highly specialized businesses usually face less competition but have to target their limited audience much more carefully.

Case Study 5

Name: Charles Custom Cabinets

Business Type: Custom cabinet installations

Years in Business: 22

Gross Revenue: $3,200,000

Employees: 16

Circumstances

Charles has been in business for more than two decades. Business is great, and he meets every advertising sales rep with the same objection: "I'm already too busy." Charles is considering cutting out all of his advertising. He does all kinds of direct mailings and all of the business and home expos, he dominates the local directories, and he has a small ad agency running radio and television ads for him on a regular basis. The home and garden section of his local newspaper always runs one of his sharp ads. What should Charles do?

Marketing Solution

If Charles cuts out his advertising completely, he will likely still stay in business for some time. However, he will begin to lose customers and referrals from attrition over time. It seems that Charles has some room for cuts, but disappearing completely from the consumers' eyes may not be a good idea.

Charles cuts his radio and television program and stops making the coupon offers. He buys two high-traffic billboards and displays a powerful but simple branding message. He cuts down his Yellow Pages ads, but he still keeps a presence with a newer ad that features quality over cost. Charles gets in touch with a popular local home magazine that allows him to be a contributing writer who has a column about interior home improvements. He in turn buys a beautiful ad within the publication. One of the talk-radio stations in town sells one-hour blocks on Saturday mornings. Charles buys a spot and has a weekly call-in show dedicated to home improvement.

Charles has been in business long enough to have strong branding in his local market. Without disappearing completely, he is able to cut back on his advertising somewhat while strengthening his image as an expert in his area. Charles goes on to have continued success and also enjoys sharing his knowledge with his new advertorial pieces.

Case Study 6

Name: Dr. Fallon Family Medicine

Business Type: Family-practice doctor's office

Years in Business: 9

Gross Revenue: $950,000

Employees: 9

Circumstances

Dr. Fallon has a strong family practice that she built from the ground up. While her patient level grows at a slow pace, she would like to see more new clients. She never felt that marketing could do much for her business, as most people came in as personal or insurance referrals. Wanting her business to grow so that she may add another doctor or physician's assistant, she looks for a solution.

Marketing Solution

Dr. Fallon is listed in the local Yellow Pages but decides to increase her online ranking on some search engines and directories. She assumes correctly that people like to do research before finding a new doctor, and much of that can be done online. The listings will bring potential clients to her website, which is complete and full of accolades from clients and other professionals.

There are many social events and fundraisers in her community, so Dr. Fallon starts to participate in and donate to more local charity events. Her image of caring crosses over to brand her practice in the same light. At the same time, her presence in the community helps people put a face and a personality with her name.

Dr. Fallon also takes out an ad in a quarterly family health publication put out by her local paper. This publication will help continue to brand her practice and build on the relationships she has already created in the community.

Professionals of all kinds can benefit from marketing in one way or another. By keeping herself out there both in the literal and in the marketing sense, she will be at the front of people's minds when they are considering changing doctors or finding one for the first time. People may still look at lists provided by their insurance company, but Dr. Fallon's name will certainly stand out because of her marketing strategy.

Action Plan

The next step in *90 Days to Success Marketing and Advertising Your Small Business* will be meeting with your advertising sales reps. It is important for you to figure out where your business is and where you want it to go through your marketing strategy. However, your plans may change after meeting with reps, learning specifics about the mediums in your market, and pricing out programs.

It is important for you to answer the following questions to build an effective marketing program. You will uncover gaps in your needs and even find places where there may be some waste.

✓ What is your business goal?

✓ What forms of directional advertising does your business already have? What new directional avenues might help you reach your goals?

✓ What forms of creative advertising does your business already have? What new branding mediums might help you reach your goals?

✓ What forms of call-to-action advertising does your business already have? What new CTA products might help you reach your goals?

✓ Where do people find your contact information when they need to call you?

✓ How well branded is your company?

✓ What are the most aggressive call-to-action offers you can make?

✓ What do you currently spend on advertising?

✓ Where are you getting a good return on your investment?

✓ Where are you getting a poor return on your investment or even a loss?

✓ How do you conceptualize your marketing program?

✓ Are there opportunities for you to compete for new business in the Yellow Pages or online?

✓ Are you looking for immediate results from call-to-action advertising, are you trying to strengthen your brand, or a combination of both?

Chapter 6

Sales Reps, Contracts, and Negotiations

- Sales Compensation
- Salespeople
- Contracts and Negotiations
- Contracts
- Action Plan

The phone rings. "Hi, this is Tim Timminson from the *Timminson Times*. We're running a special for new advertisers to our publication, and I want to offer you a full-color half-page ad for just $249!" It's the fourth call today from a local advertising sales rep. You just met with your payroll salesperson, a distributor, and a staffing representative; the last thing you want to do is take this call.

I've been there on both sides of the phone. As an advertising sales rep, I needed to have a unique and enticing approach to gain my potential customers' attention. I knew that I was somewhere toward the bottom of the totem pole for most business owners, and I needed to convince them that I could play a crucial part in growing their business. After a business owner meets with three other salespeople providing solutions for immediate and tangible needs, it's hard to sell something a little less tangible that is very difficult to quantify. When a business owner meets with a payroll rep, he's looking for cost-effective solutions for managing his payroll. Every company relies on supply people to deliver the goods necessary to keep their business moving forward. Staffing agencies can provide you with employees almost immediately for temporary or permanent positions. On the other hand, when an advertising sales rep comes in, she's selling a product that may or may not get the company more business and a product that will be difficult to track either way.

On the flipside, as a business owner I wanted to get the maximum amount of information out of those salespeople with the minimum amount of interruption to my day. I knew that even though not every medium was right for my company, these people had competitive information on the market I was working in and variable solutions for me to implement my marketing strategy.

The reality is that advertising salespeople and businesses have one of the most unique relationships in the world of small business. A good sales rep and a willing businessperson can both benefit from a properly founded relationship.

Sales Compensation

Like most other salespeople, advertising sales reps are generally compensated through commission. They're paid a percentage of the value of the product they sell you. Although they may be looking to grow your business, their pay is based on their results, not yours. If one rep sells a $10,000 program that fails, he's still going to make a lot more money on that transaction than the rep who sells a $1,000 program that delivers results to the customer. All reps will tell you that their goal is to help you sustain and grow your company. The real challenge is to decipher the information they're giving you, knowing that their ulterior motive is to also make money.

Did you notice how I specified that the $10,000 rep made more money than the $1,000 rep *on that specific transaction*? That's because the $1,000 salesperson will likely make more money over the course of his or her career. Although there are a lot of churn-and-burn temporary salespeople out there looking to make a quick buck, there are some who understand that their line of business is just like yours. They have to do a good job in order to get your repeat business and referrals. If the $1,000 rep improved your business, you're likely to listen to his or her recommendations the next time around and possibly give a positive referral to another business owner. If you blew $10,000 with someone on a failed program, first of all you probably won't see this person again, and secondly, you'd slam the door in his face if he did decide to show up.

Some companies will pay their sales force better commissions on new advertisers. This creates a bit of a divide between the medium and its employees. They want new business for the same reason you do. It helps them grow their bottom line with the added sales and anticipated repeat business. Because salespeople are frequently paid better on these kinds of sales, they tend to over-sell new advertisers. Ultimately, being oversold on a product can cause it to fail. A sandwich shop duped into buying a full-page ad in a newspaper would likely never come back when comparing results to cost. If they were sold an appropriately sized ad for a small takeout restaurant, they'd be more likely to continue the ad for an extended amount of time. In the case of the full-page ad, the business took a hit, and the paper lost a customer, but the salesperson got a one-time huge commission check.

Have a concept of your marketing strategy *before* you meet with salespeople.

This can make your decision as a business owner even more difficult. If you over-commit, you may not see a return on your investment. If you try to counter an overzealous rep with an under-commitment, you may not see results, and you may lose confidence in their product. As stated in earlier chapters, this is why it's extremely important to have a concept of your marketing strategy before you meet with salespeople.

Some companies offer different incentives to their sales force for selling new or different forms of media they're offering. A radio sales rep for a station with great listenership might be given special incentives to sell advertising space on the station's new or failing website. If you have a weak website and you do not have a business that could benefit from being on their site, it doesn't mean the rep won't try to sell it to you.

Although the commissions can be high, advertising sales has a very high turnover rate compared to other traditional sales positions. Many mediums have a practice of hiring a large number of professional and energetic people, throwing them right into the field, and then seeing who sticks. And although many people have great success in advertising sales, it is often considered an entry-level position. If someone interviews well and has some general office experience, it's usually enough to get that person a shot. Some pick it up and understand the mutual benefits provided to their customers, employer, and own paycheck, but a vast majority tend to burn out in a short time. This is why it's important for you to learn to identify certain types of salespeople.

Salespeople

Now that you understand the basics of how salespeople are compensated, let's take a few minutes to discuss some of the types of salespeople you may encounter.

Fly-by-Night Salespeople

I'll start with the worst of the potential salespeople you could meet with so that I can leave you with a better feeling about advertising sales reps by the end of this chapter. These are the people you have to watch out for. They will sell you anything and everything to make as much money as possible, as quickly as possible. They tend to stay with companies for less than a year as they burn through as many potential advertisers as possible. While they're trying to make a lot of money, they also look at their position as a stepping-stone to something better. Although most companies do everything they can to prevent fraud, if anyone is going to go for it, it's these kinds of employees.

Watch out for boastful reps who can't back up their claims. They may tell you they have great numbers and have helped a lot of businesses grow, but you'll be hard-pressed to get them to give you any references. They tend to be flashy both on a personal and on a professional level. Their favorite type of close is the assumptive close. Many seasoned sales reps will do this with clients they have worked with for a long time, but this is not something that should happen when you work with someone for the first time.

> Beware of unfamiliar sales reps who use an assumptive-close strategy.

An assumptive close is when the sales rep presents the idea and expects you to sign on the dotted line with no discussion or objections. A good rep will answer all of your questions and take your concerns seriously; a bad, fly-by-night rep will likely talk down to you and use guilt tactics to get you to sign. If you ever get a sales rep who makes you feel uncomfortable or who you simply do not trust, don't be afraid to ask to work with someone different. You don't have to address the sales rep in question; just get in contact with a sales manager.

Also, don't feel as if you're taking food out of the sales rep's mouth. If you provided bad service to one of your customers, wouldn't you expect the customer to find someone else to provide a like product or service?

Rookie Burnouts

These people are similar to the fly-by-night reps but usually are not loaded with as many self-serving intentions. They tend to have some people skills and a bit of professional ability, but they completely lack any knowledge of the product and its potential. If they have any need for a serious income, they, too, do not last for much more than a year.

You can often get rock-bottom prices from rookie-burnout reps looking for a quick sale.

The bad side is that rookie burnouts do their own company a disservice. They may be working for one of the most effective mediums in your area, but you'd never know it by their lackluster presentation skills. They often seek out very small sales in the hopes of simply making a sale. I can't tell you how many of these employees I worked with at a particular Yellow Pages company. They'd go on a new business call, come back with a couple bold listings, and consider it a success. Most of those advertisers would see little reason to continue a paid program with us the following year because they didn't get any tangible results.

The good thing is that you can usually get exactly what you want out of your sales rep. These reps will turn into very quiet order-takers if you already know what you want. It's also very easy to get the rock-bottom best price out of them. They sell based on dollar value and will immediately hit rock bottom for you. This is good if you have an idea of what kind of program you're looking into, but you don't expect to be educated or consulted on any level. You'll get what you want quickly and quietly, but you may miss out on some other decent opportunities. Also, don't get too attached, because these rookie burnouts likely won't be your rep for much longer.

Mid-Career Salespeople

Watch out for the negotiating skills of mid-career sales-people. They can be quite persuasive.

Many people do have success in advertising sales. They understand how to educate their clients and build effective advertising programs. These employees can range from relatively new to up to 10 years or more of experience with a company. Although they find success in what they do, they often move on to management or other high-end sales positions, such as pharmaceutical sales, financial sales, and so on. You'll be able to spot these kinds of reps quickly, because they will ask a lot of questions and take a legitimate interest in what you're trying to accomplish. They can talk to you about other businesses they've worked with and share success stories to help you overcome any objections you may have. They will also quantify their marketing suggestions and tie them into what you've told them and what they can provide.

If you end up working with a rep like this, hold onto him or her. These reps might not be around forever, but they can be a very useful resource. Because of their success in their medium, they will often try to up-sell you. Fortunately, they will usually be able to back up their strategy, but they will also gracefully move in a different direction as you see fit. The only thing you should watch out for is their negotiating ability. These reps may be so good at their job that they can convince you to change your marketing strategy completely. Be sure not to make any on-the-spot decisions if the rep asks you to do something drastic, and always calculate your risk and other options.

Career Advertising Salespeople

These are the most successful advertising salespeople you will ever come across. They know their product inside out, as well as many of the other mediums in your area. They've built lasting relationships with many other business owners and have done so by helping them implement successful marketing strategies. They've usually been with the same company for more than five years and have no intention of going anywhere else. Often earning more than their managers, they see no need to make any changes in their careers.

Career advertising salespeople can be useful in plotting your marketing goals.

You can count on career advertising salespeople to help you achieve your goals, as long as their medium is the backbone of your campaign. They usually will not work with small-level accounts unless it's a referral or a favor for one of their clients. Unfortunately, some companies lack anyone fitting this description, so you may never run into someone with this kind of experience. If you do, these reps can tell you success and failure stories for all kinds of businesses and mediums in your area. I would never suggest blindly following sales reps of any kind, but these people in particular can make great marketing co-pilots.

Contracts and Negotiations

No matter who you end up working with, you'll have to engage in some form of negotiation. Whether it's negotiating price or product, there will be some back and forth.

Base your advertising decisions on the anticipated effectiveness of a program.

Meeting with as many salespeople as possible can help your business in two very specific ways. First of all, good sales reps can educate you on your market, competition, strategies, and so on. Second, having all kinds of competing offers can help when it comes to negotiation. You'll learn the pricing for similar mediums and be able to compare and contrast coverage and effectiveness. Why pay $2,000 for an ad in a coupon magazine when another is offering the same coverage for $1,200? Maybe that $2,000 is not their rock-bottom price yet, and now that you're comparing it to a like product, they'll be willing to deal. If they're not willing to deal, you're forcing them to qualify the added price. Maybe they have more circulation, or maybe they use a higher-quality paper.

Your advertising decisions should not be based on dollar value alone; rather, they should be based on the anticipated effectiveness of the program. That being said, no one wants to pay $200 for a television spot that a better negotiator is paying $190 for. The following suggestions (which I'm trying my hardest not to refer to as "tricks") can help you make sure you're getting the best price. Remember, honesty is always the best way of doing business, but there's nothing wrong with withholding your plans to fish for the best rate.

High-Frequency Publications

Showing some tentativeness to your sales rep could end up getting you a better deal on your advertising.

If you're considering running an ad in any kind of print publication that comes out on a monthly, weekly, or daily basis, there is usually a special rate card for discounts based on how many publications you agree to. If you only want to run something once, there is something usually referred to as an *open* rate. A quarter page in a monthly magazine may be $900 based on running your ad once. As you increase the frequency, the rate improves. Usually the rate bottoms out at a *contract* rate, which implies you'll run for an entire year or over their top threshold. That same quarter page ad might be $850 for 2 to 6 runs, $800 for 7 to 11 runs, and $750 for a full 12-month commitment. The reality is, you should never pay more than the contract rate, even if you're only going to run your ad for one month.

Although I never suggest "trying out" any kind of advertising without a serious commitment, you should still use your tentativeness to secure a guaranteed low rate. You and I know an ad in a magazine will not reach its peak effectiveness in one month, but your sales rep doesn't need to know how educated you are on the matter. Make the price point the deal breaker and watch the rep make you "this one-time super-duper deal."

Volume Discounts

Similar to high-frequency discounts, some salespeople will offer you discounts for running more ads. This is seen most often with Yellow Pages, online banner ads, and billboards. You can run your ad in multiple headings, in more places online, or on more billboards for deeper discounts. When you let your sales reps present various programs within their product, let them—and even advise them to—build something with a much larger volume than you anticipate running. Once they make their offers, take the pricing from the higher volume and ask whether you can get the same discount on a somewhat smaller program. For example, if a billboard sales rep offers you four street-level posters for $2,000 ($500 each) but can offer you 12 street-level posters for $4,000 ($300 each), try to negotiate for the lower rate even with the lower volume. In this case, I would ask for four street-level posters for $1,200. It's an available rate based on a higher volume, so you're not asking them to lose their shirts, but you're attempting to save yourself $800 per month.

Up-Sell Discounts

This is one of the most obnoxious offers that I see on a stunningly frequent basis. Fortunately for you, this offer in itself is a great way for you to get a deep discount on the product you've already decided you want. Let's say you've met with a Yellow Pages sales rep, and after much negotiation, you've agreed to buy a half-page advertisement for $800 per month.

SURPRISE!

"For new advertisers / because we're at the end of the sales canvass / because you've been such a loyal customer / because there's a full moon—we're offering you a free upgrade to the next size up, which is known as a double column or a 2/3-page ad, for free! Now your $800 will buy you an even larger ad! Isn't that wonderful?"

Beware the up-sell discount. It is rarely as good as they make it sound.

No, it's not wonderful. What they're really saying is that you could have gotten the half-page ad you wanted for less money. If you had decided on a quarter-page ad for $620, they would have upgraded you to a half page. So now instead of paying $620 for the ad you wanted, you're paying $800 for an ad that may be larger than what you need.

If this happens, demand what you already agreed to for a lower price. They will try to fight back and say the half page is the smallest one they will give the free upgrade to, and so on. Stick to your guns—this will usually work.

Agency Discounts

It can be difficult to get significant discounts from radio and television companies because their rates are usually tied to a very specific formula based on ratings. This agency discount trick—er, suggestion—can work with some other mediums as well. Many large companies do their media buying through advertising agencies. If a large national company wants to buy a $100 spot on a local radio station, they will pay their agency $100 for the spot, and the agency will receive a commission—usually around 15 percent from the radio station—by paying only $85 for the spot.

After you've had some varying spots priced out for you, ask them whether there are any deeper discounts they can find for each ad. If they don't bend, ask them about the agency discount. Let them know that you know ad agencies get better rates. They'll explain to you that the 15-percent discount is in lieu of paying a sales rep a commission. The reality is that, even if they're not aware of it, the liaison between the agency and the station is still being paid a commission. It's limited, but it still exists. If you get your sales rep thinking about these discounts and talking to his or her sales managers, you may be surprised to see what they come back with.

New-Business Discounts

As a loyal customer, you shouldn't feel shy about asking for new-business discounts. Why not?

Many advertising mediums will make better offers to new customers to get them to try their product. If you are new to the publication, enjoy your discount! If you're a loyal customer and have already been doing business with this company, you may feel a little betrayed. Likely, your sales rep is not going to tell you about any new-business discounts if you're not a new business. You best bet is to occasionally ask your sales reps whether there are any special discounts going on. They may inform you of their usual offers, but don't be afraid to pry and ask whether there's a new-business discount. Remind them of your loyalty and see whether they will kindly give you some similar discounts.

Cross-Medium Discounts

Many companies are starting to branch out and offer their advertisers other marketing solutions beyond what they're used to. Your local newspaper may also have a magazine, a coupon mailer or insert, direct mail, a website, or something similar. You should expect to get a discount for doing business with them across their varying revenue streams, but you should also try to have them honor similar discounts even if you don't always take advantage of all their offers. If you get a 10-percent discount for duplicating your newspaper ad as a banner ad online, you should ask for that same discount even if you're not always running online. If you simply ask, you may even be able to secure the discount without running online.

Advance-Pay Discounts

Many advertising companies will expect you to prepay a portion of your bill, make monthly installments, or remit payment upon delivery of their service. Sometimes, if you offer to pay your bill in full for the duration of your contract (a full year, a full run of commercials, and so on), you will be given a slight pay-in-full discount. This can save you some money, but I only suggest doing this with companies you're comfortable with. If you've been in the same church bulletin for six years, you've probably gotten a good enough response to know you want to continue your program. If you have enough working capital, why not save a decent percentage off your bill? However, if you aren't going to get a discount for paying a large amount in advance, don't bother. You're giving them an interest-free loan on your money!

If you know you plan to stay with an advertising campaign, check to see whether any advance-pay discounts are available.

Apples-to-Apples Discounts

As I mentioned earlier in this chapter, it can be beneficial to meet with as many different salespeople as possible. If one direct-mail company is offering to mail a postcard for $500 per thousand homes, and another is offering the same thing for $450, play them against each other. There is nothing wrong with giving people the chance to meet or beat their competitors' prices. If you were about to make a deal with one of your customers and they were offered a better price from your competition, might you budge?

Apples-to-Oranges Discounts

Even if you're not comparing the same medium, it may be worth your time to share competitive information with your sales rep. You might get a better price for your billboard if the rep sees you find more value in an aggressively priced television campaign. Tell the rep you're still up in the air and making your decision and that you'd like him to make his best offer before you decide whom to advertise with. The reality is you may end up with both, but you want to ensure the best price possible.

General Suggestions

Try not to sign on the spot if the contract is not legitimately time sensitive. If your sales rep gets any sense that you may have your doubts, he or she may present some better offers to entice you to sign.

Ask other businesspeople what they're paying for their ads. Of course, these should be people you're comfortable with, but you can often help each other out if one of you is getting a better deal than the other.

If you ever see a deal that's simply too good to be true, it probably is. Struggling mediums often lower their prices in a last-ditch effort to stay afloat. Also, you never know whether your sales rep has made a mistake or, even worse, is trying to pull one over on you.

The larger the company you're dealing with, the less likely you are to negotiate a deal. Sales reps for large national companies often have less leeway and less control over the pricing. This doesn't mean you should rake your local or regional advertising companies over the coals, but understand that there may be varying limitations.

Even if you think you've gotten a deal, do not show your cards. If there are any further discounts to get, they're worth getting.

If you keep a fair and open line communication with your sales rep, you can get a reasonable discount, and your rep will usually inform you of any cost-saving measures. Just remember, it can't hurt to ask. Try any of the discount suggestions I have given or come up with some of your own.

You may not like the process of negotiating, and you might even feel as if you're getting more than enough value from your advertising program. But consider this: You may have been in business for years with multiple employees and an aggressive advertising budget of $200,000 per year. If you saved yourself just a dime on every dollar, even if the program is working, you could end up with another $20,000 to be spent on something else.

Remember, these salespeople are trying to make a living, too. They need to make sales to make commissions, and their employers need to make a profit. Understand that the intention of the relationship between a small business and an advertising company is to be mutually beneficial. You shouldn't expect to get 1,000 television commercials for $500, just as you shouldn't expect your brand-new car to cost $500.

Contracts

Your salesperson is providing the contract to be signed, but these documents offer you a fair amount of protection as well. Some will show what kinds of refunds you're entitled to if certain parts of your ad campaign come up short or in error. They also guarantee what you're entitled to. If you make a "gentleman's agreement" with a handshake and a check, there's no guarantee the company is going to deliver what they've told you. If you're supposed to get a half-page ad, 200 commercials, or 10,000 postcards, get it in writing. If there's an error by the salesperson or their company or an intentional misrepresentation, the contract you sign is the only thing you have to protect yourself.

Get everything in writing, and be sure to read the fine print!

Read over your contract and be sure you understand the fine print. It may seem tedious, but it will save you a potential headache down the road. Make sure all of the variables you've discussed appear on paper exactly as you discussed them. If there is any variance or discrepancy or anything that seems uncertain, do not sign the contract. If you're told they'll fix or clarify your contract later, do not sign the contract.

This may irritate your sales rep, and they will certainly try to tell you otherwise, but be certain to have a hard copy of your contract as soon as you sign it. With today's technology, many salespeople are doing business on their laptops with signature pads. They have the ability to go back into these documents and make changes at any time. Although you can trust 99 out of 100 salespeople to be relatively honest, you must conduct your business with them in a paper contract, especially if you're going to make any advance payments. If your rep tells you they don't offer paper contracts, end your meeting and have the rep talk to his sales manager. They'll produce a contract.

If you do business with an online or out-of-town provider, make an attempt to complete your transaction with the addition of faxed or scanned contracts. Sometimes you may not even be speaking with a person, and your only choice is point and click, but the more paperwork the better.

I must reiterate that most advertising sales reps and their employers are out to make money by providing you with a product that works. I had to paint them with broad strokes to educate you on the process, but most of your experiences with these people will more than likely turn out positive.

Action Plan

It's time to put your marketing strategy into action! Although it may seem like a lot of redundant work, it's of the utmost importance that you follow these steps. By taking meetings with reps from all kinds of competing media, you'll expose yourself to a wider range of opportunities, you'll learn more, and you'll have far more ammunition when it comes to negotiations.

✓ Get on the phone and set appointments with as many sales reps from as many varying and competitive mediums as possible. If you want to successfully market and advertise your business, it is important that you make these meetings a priority.

✓ Use the marketing plans you have been brainstorming to dictate the direction of your meetings.

✓ Allow and/or ask for your sales rep's full presentation. Reps may think they're saving you time by skipping some of it, but this is a learning experience.

✓ Collect offers or contracts in writing to start getting a grasp on your advertising budget.

✓ Reconnect with your salespeople and voice your thoughts to work on negotiating.

✓ Determine which offers will help you achieve your marketing goals at the most reasonable price.

✓ Start the discussion with your sales reps on effective content, messages, and offers, which we'll cover in the next chapter.

Chapter 7

Content and Offers

- Ad Copy
- Commercials
- Branding
- Medium Notes
- Action Plan

If you're a curious member of an advertising agency or you're a marketing major, you're going to hate me for this chapter. Contrary to popular belief driven by marketing elitists, the content and design of an ad are second to an effective program. You could have the most beautiful award-winning advertisement created by the most expensive ad agency in town, but it's not going to get you results unless it's implemented in an effective fashion. Ads with strong offers run frequently and in the correct places will do a lot more for your business than a highbrow Fortune 500 ad created by a self-proclaimed marketing genius.

All of that being said, what goes into your commercials, print ads, and mailings *does* play an important role in bringing your business results.

Ad Copy

All print advertisements are built around content or ad copy. This is what makes up the bulk of your message. There is usually a featured headline or tagline with supporting information and sometimes an offer.

Taglines

Most print advertisements contain a tagline.

Taglines are the featured idea of a single ad or an entire marketing strategy. A business looking to provide low-cost services while relying on volume to turn a profit might do some version of the generic "Lowest Prices in Town!" A high-end provider might consider a version of "Highest Quality in Town!"

Be sure your ad content supports your tagline.

These taglines set the agenda for the rest of the advertisement. If you use quality to draw people in, continue with that theme within your bullet points. Talk about the products you use, the high levels of satisfaction, and so on. Businesses make big mistakes when the rest of the ad content doesn't support their taglines. If you claim to have the highest quality in town, but then you spend the rest of your ad space talking about price matching and lowest prices guaranteed, consumers will not take your message as seriously and will have a difficult time making associations with your business when they're ready to make a buying decision.

My initial examples were generic and, quite honestly, should be avoided in the verbiage. Consumers are flooded with all kinds of advertising, and these messages have lost a lot of their power. So instead of "Lowest Prices in Town!" a jeweler could tag his print ads with "Home of the Hundred-Dollar Diamond!" Of course, the jeweler may sell something that's a fraction of a carat for a hundred dollars, but the tagline sets the tone for the ad as well as the jeweler's business. If another local jeweler wanted the "Highest Quality in Town!" theme, she should focus on something other than price. "World-Renowned for Our Hand-Cut Diamonds!" might be a better idea for a jeweler going for big-ticket sales. People will understand that they may be paying more for a well-respected, high-quality product.

Bullet Points

Your ads don't have to be laid out in a bullet-point format, but I refer to the bulk content of ads as such. These are little tidbits of information about your business that you want to share with the world. It's important to focus on things that will set your business aside from the competition. Try to avoid space fillers, such as "Free Estimates" or "Professional Staff," that your advertising sales rep may push to fill up space and speed up the process. These kinds of broad statements cause your ad to blend in with the rest of your competition. Better versions of the same statements might read as, "Detailed Estimates with Line-Item Pricing" or "Staff Participates in Continuing Education"—anything to give more substance to the statement.

Make points that have substance; avoid using empty phrasing to fill space.

This is why it's important to pay attention to your competitor's advertisements. If they all offer five-year guarantees, can you offer a six-year guarantee? If everyone offers free consultations, use your space on something more unique, such as the fact that you offer home appointments or you have weekend hours available. Although your bullet points are not meant to draw in people the same way taglines are, it's still important for them to have a level of uniqueness.

Visuals

Most print mediums will offer you photo images in your advertisement. Just like taglines, these images are meant to draw people into your advertisement. Also, they need to be relevant to your business so they, too, can set the tone for your ad and your business's offerings. People *do* judge books by their covers, so it's important to put some thought into your images. Just as your sales rep may push generic ad content on you, he'll do the same with images. If you're a personal trainer, just putting a clip of a barbell or a treadmill in your ad is a waste of time. Find something with more power and emotion that will make people wonder about the content of your ad. A good idea might be to include a super close-up of a face straining during a workout. It will look unusual enough to draw people in, and it will set people up for an ad for a service where they will be pushed to their limits by a trainer.

Many ads will contain pictures of business owners or a group photo of everyone in the company. This can be a good idea, but sales reps more often use it as a ploy to go after business owners' egos. The personal trainer might love the idea of his picture in a local magazine for everyone to gawk at. But what if that personal trainer weighs 300 pounds? Sure, he could be healthier than most people around, but the fact of the matter is that people do make judgments, whether consciously or subconsciously, and a large personal trainer doesn't necessarily inspire confidence that he will be able to get his clients in slim, healthy shape. It can be tough to look at yourself or your staff members and determine how consumers will judge you, so you may be better off erring on the side of a different image for your ads.

Be careful of stock images. It's often easy to tell whether an image is from some random database. If you're a small-town accountant and your ad features a guy in a sky-scraper office, it's not going to feel as local or legit. Consider (carefully) using your own picture in your own office or possibly a picture of a consumer who's clearly troubled over her taxes or bookkeeping. I once used a stock photo of a beautiful home with intricate colors, and people kept asking me where that particular house was. After I explained that it was a stock image, they clearly wondered why I hadn't used a photo of my own.

Offers

Any medium can make an offer in some form, but print ads seem void without one. Whether the offer is a coupon or a statement, a call to action can double the duties of creative and directional ads.

Coupons work best in mediums we've already determined to be call-to-action ads, as people expect to see them there. It's important to determine what your competitors are offering so that you can better or at least duplicate what they're making public. Dollar values and free offers work best, but if you prefer to work with percentages, make sure it's at least 15 percent. If your competition is offering $3 off a $15 product, offering a lesser percentage can kill the results of your ad if all other things are relatively equal.

Making an offer in a nontraditional call-to-action ad can be a little more difficult. A coupon in the middle of a high-end magazine or a Yellow Pages directory may cause people to shy away. Instead, you might try something like "Call and ask how to get a free ..." or "$30 off with the mention of this ad." The simple lack of hash marks or dotted lines designating a coupon means consumers cannot cut out your offer—and believe it or not, they will look at it in a better light.

Make an offer in your call-to-action print ad, whether by coupon or by statement.

Commercials

Television and radio commercials share a lot of the same features as print ads. They need a main idea or a tagline, content or bullet points, and a strong visual (or audio) draw to the commercial. The only difference is that you control the direction of the consumption of your information. This gives you a unique opportunity to hook consumers to draw in their attention and then deliver the information with a better absorption rate.

To hook listeners or viewers, you have to latch onto their emotional needs. Tell a brief story that can address a need your potential customers may have or may foresee having in the future. "If your car breaks down on the highway, who's the only mechanic who can guarantee a tow within one hour or it's free?

Latch onto the emotional needs of listeners or viewers when you're creating a commercial.

Johnson and Sons Auto." Whether that's an opening to a commercial on radio or television, you've hooked your potential clientele. Most people deal with their car breaking down at some point, so most people are listening. They learn that Johnson and Sons will get to them in less than an hour or the tow is free! You've presented a hook, a main idea, and an offer in less than 10 seconds. Now you can focus the rest of the commercial on your services, products, and so on and be assured that you have a captive audience.

Be sure your name is heard or seen throughout the commercial—don't wait until the end to tell the viewer or listener who you are!

If this was a television commercial, you could create obvious and powerful images depicting someone breaking down on the side of the road and making a call to Johnson and Sons, who then show up promptly. A radio ad could use the same story with some engine sounds and a call of desperation.

Commercials are meant for branding, so it's important for your name to appear or be heard several times. Too often, I see a decent commercial that waits until the last second to announce who is offering the product or service. It may not seem normal to you or even your television rep, but consider keeping your name and/or logo on the screen at all times during the commercial. People can view your name in a static location while getting the idea of the commercial. When you're watching television and a small ad pops up about a different program than the one you're watching, you're usually able to continue with your show but ingest the branding message too.

Jingles

Musical jingles can leave a lasting impression on consumers and can play a hand in branding a business. A regular commercial about a visit to a chiropractor isn't going to stick in your mind verbatim for very long, no matter how many times you hear it. However, if this chiropractor's message is delivered in a jingle, the commercial will stick (sometimes to a fault!) in people's heads for a much longer time.

This may sound like the perfect way to get the most out of your radio or television ad, but jingles take a long time to maximize their effectiveness. Also, there are many added costs to production, and jingles require a lot more airtime to become a "song" that people remember. Also, it's difficult to make any kind of direct offer in a jingle so they must be used purely for branding. *Years* down the road, if your jingle has caught on, you can tone it down and leave it in the background while you play a content-based commercial over the familiar song. When working with someone to produce a jingle, make sure it's unusually memorable. Very firm and ranging notes make it easier for people to remember the jingle. Also, if it sounds like normal music, it's not going to be as memorable as that cheesy commercial that's already been running through your head as you began to read this section....

Branding

As discussed in earlier chapters, the purpose of branding is to give your business front-of-the-mind placement when people are thinking about your type of product or service. Branding on the local level is all about consistency and repetitive messages. Think of that "annoying" car dealer or attorney whose commercial you cannot seem to escape while watching television. You may find these ads invasive, but you can certainly recall these businesses in particular. Even if these messages are driven so hard into your mind that you choose to avoid these businesses, I'm sure you know people who have sought after their services. I'm also willing to bet that you've been seeing these commercials for years, thus proving the success that those businesses have had and the effectiveness of their seemingly "annoying" branding messages.

Branding is about consistency and repetition.

Think of the humor and creativity of Super Bowl commercials you've seen in the past. Now try to recall what national brands were tied to those messages. Although there is very little that can be drawn from a national campaign for a localized small business, you can see how ineffective messages can be if they're not done in a repetitive and effective manner.

Imagine two new dentists in your town are competing for business. One hires the most expensive advertising agency to design a magazine advertisement that he plans to run in a high-end publication. The agency creates a beautiful ad for Dr. Stevens with great color and a powerful message that really makes you think. The ad even wins an award for outstanding creativity! The ad changes each month, creating a linear story for people who subscribe to the magazine.

The second dentist decides to do all of his advertising buying on his own. Dr. Dillon meets with his Yellow Pages rep, a billboard salesman, and someone from a local radio station. He agrees to run ads with all three of these mediums. He informs them all that in a few days, he will send them the main idea of his ad content via email. Several days pass, and the dentist is writing an email to his sales representatives. In the middle of the email he's interrupted by his wife, who wants to know what he wants to order for takeout from a Chinese restaurant. He responds, "Dr. Dillon Loves Duck!" in a playful manner. Unbeknownst to him, he sends the bold statement to his sales reps by accident. Because they are intimidated by Dr. Dillon, they are too nervous to challenge the dentist's email, and they run with the idea. (Of course this would never happen because of proofs, common sense by the production teams, and so on, but this wacky example will pay off if you stick with me!)

Next month, four billboards go up across town with pictures of ducks and the statement, "Dr. Dillon, DDS, the Dentist Who Loves Ducks!" Over the radio, a repetitive commercial airs throughout the day. "Dr. Dillon, DDS, is a dentist who loves ducks! Call now for an exam!" The commercial opens and closes with ducks quacking in the background. The Yellow Pages hits the streets, and there people find a full-page ad with Dr. Dillon's caricature hugging a cartoon duck. The bold headline reads, "Dr. Dillon, DDS, Loves Ducks!" His contact info is listed below.

Of course this is an extreme example, but it's not quite as far out as you might think. Ducks and dentistry have little (if anything) to do with each other. However, I'm willing to bet that if you queried a thousand people in the streets of this town and asked them to name some local dentists, Dr. Dillon would be high on that list. While Dr. Stevens ran a beautiful ad that made much more sense, Dr. Dillon had more success at branding his practice. People who were moved by Dr. Stevens's ad may take him more seriously, but a far larger portion of the population would likely shrug their shoulders or snicker at the nonsensical ads that Dr. Dillon ran and make a call.

Next year, the two dentists decide to merge their practices and share notes on their marketing strategies....

Although this may have been a nonsensical example, the purpose was to show you that repetition and consistency are crucial when you set out to brand your business. Let's take a look at a more serious approach to branding.

Visuals

Regardless of the mediums, it's important to have a consistent look across your marketing strategy as a whole. If you use green and gold in your billboards, use green and gold in your direct mail. If you provide shirts or uniforms for your employees, go for green and gold. Signs, trucks, even television commercials can be enhanced if they continue with the same color scheme. Businesses with logos or icons should incorporate them into all visual mediums. Any other associated imagery should remain consistent as well. If you own a housecleaning service that caters to seniors, keep similar images of seniors in all of your market-ing regardless of the type. Using the same model can also help, if you have that kind of access.

Be consistent in your look across your marketing strategy as a whole.

Message

If you can sum up the main idea of your business's offerings in a short sentence or phrase, stick to it and use it over and over again. "Williams's Wells—Drilled in a Day!" would be a great short tag for all portions of Williams's marketing strategy. The headline of their Yellow Pages ad, the opening and closing of their commer-cials, and even their direct-mail pieces should be branded with this simple yet effective phrase. People will recognize Williams's Wells as a well driller, and Williams's will be associated with prompt one-day service.

Besides running with a similar tagline, using similar content can also help. If a tire-shop owner features his 20-bay garage in his television commercial, it would be a good idea for his newspaper ad to make mention of the same factor. If someone sees his commercial on television twice and then sees the newspaper ad once, he's still branded that one specific aspect of his business

Use a similar tagline and similar ad content across all your marketing mediums.

three times to this particular customer. If the television commercial featured the 20-bay garage but his newspaper ad only flaunted the shop's wide range of brands, the overall message would be weakened. A smart move would be to keep both key points to his business featured in all of his mediums.

Offers

Offers are intended to call people to action on the spot. However, having a repetitive offer can produce branding effects. As a painting contractor, I offered a free deck staining with any full exterior paint job. Although the intention of the coupon and offer was to persuade people to make a buying decision, the offer itself became part of my branding. We were known as a painting company who would stain your deck for free when it was time to paint your house. I included it in a coupon magazine, along with Yellow Pages and a billboard program, with a good amount of success.

Medium Notes

I'd like to share some specific content notes for each medium to help you build a stronger marketing program. Also, I've included some examples of effective ads for each type.

Yellow Pages

The Yellow Pages adhere to the basic rules of print ads, but you must remember that the Yellow Pages is the one place where you are in forced direct competition with all of the other like businesses in your area. You may need to consider running some redundant information that your competition is running. If it's not in your ad, consumers don't know you do it. Your company might offer free delivery just like your competition does, but if you leave it out and people are looking for it, they'll pass by your ad. Visuals are important in Yellow Pages, just not as important as complete content. If you're in a highly competitive heading and you want one aspect of your business to stand out, then just stick to one aspect of your business.

For example, plumbing is one of the most competitive headings in the Yellow Pages. When people have a plumbing emergency, picking up the phonebook will yield the quickest results. Although all businesses should have a live person answering each call, plumbing in particular is one of those businesses where people would never leave a message in an emergency situation.

Suppose Pete the plumber has a large practice with eight plumbers and the ability to service people 24 hours a day. This is potentially his primary source of income, yet he does provide other services. Looking at the heading in his local directory, there are a lot of full-page ads already in the heading.

Pete decides to go with a full page, but he uses a unique look to draw people's eyes away from the competition. Throwing out the typical layout of ads he sees in the book, he puts a bold rectangular box in the center of his ad that simply reads, "24-hour emergency service: Direct to your home in 30 minutes or less." This box in the middle of his ad looks like a separate sub-ad, and its unique design and simple message will draw people in. Around the outside of the center box, he creates little subheadings depicting his services. One is dedicated to re-piping, another to septic, and one is for emergencies and is colored to match the center box. Another section lists his commercial services. This ad will bring in emergency callers, yet its unique look will also draw in people for other services.

Kyle is also a plumber, but he is content being a one-man service. His potential income level doesn't merit running a full-page ad, and he isn't concerned with running a one-man service. Instead of having a smaller ad that focuses on dozens of services that all of the other ads in the book include, he chooses to focus on plumbing fixtures. He buys a quarter-page ad and uses a faded toilet bowl as his backdrop. The bold and unique look draws people in and depicts one of the things on which his business focuses. His bullet points focus on sink, toilet, and tub installations, and he gives some quality factors about his business, such as, "Since 1979" and "All installations guaranteed for 10 years." Kyle will be able to bring in his primary business and will likely build a customer base for when his customers have other plumbing needs.

Newspapers

People are in reading mode when they're reading a newspaper, so feel free to present some of your content in sentence or even paragraph form. You still need to draw people in with a bold statement or image, but you may have the opportunity to get a little more reading out of your potential client. You're not competing directly with as much of your competition (unless you're in real estate or auto sales), so feel free to focus more on your business's unique qualities as opposed to completeness of content.

For example, people don't usually choose an accountant on a whim. The newspaper is a great place for people in that industry to advertise, because it tends to draw on an older, professional demographic.

Stearns Accounting has been a family business passed on for three generations. Running a successful firm since 1935 is a huge quality factor, and telling their story would create an affinity with potential clients.

The Stearns family buys an ad in the local news section of the paper. It works out to about a sixth of a page. A third of the ad is dedicated to the bold heading, "Three Generations of Accounting Expertise—Since 1935." In the bottom corner is a classic picture of their storefront from the 1940s. In the opposing corner is a portrait of the three generations side by side. The body of the ad is a simple timeline of their business and then their phone numbers.

I know what you're thinking: "Where's the offer?" Yes, an offer is always a great idea, but a company with this kind of time and experience will not make or break their business without a call to action. This is a pure branding piece capitalizing on their existing reputation and success.

As another example, Amy recently obtained her CPA and is ready to leave the firm that employs her and go out on her own. Bookkeeping has always been her area of expertise, so she wants to focus on obtaining small-business clients of her own. Amy takes out a small ad in the business section near the stock ticker. She uses a catchy tagline: "You've worked hard for your money, so manage it wisely."

Underneath the tagline is an offer for a free consultation for small-business bookkeeping. She'll review your records and build a proposal for free. This will give her potential buyers a chance to see what she has to offer without making a commitment. Amy knows that once she's in the door, she'll be able to close on their business.

Magazines

Magazines are similar to newspapers in that people will give your advertisement a little more time than they might elsewhere. However, magazines require more of a visual draw. Take advantage of bold pictures to draw in consumers. This is the one medium where visual draws outweigh taglines and offers.

For example, Cornell Custom Countertops wants to place an ad in a local leisure magazine. The magazine boasts a high-end demographic, just the one Cornell is seeking. Using creative photo editing, the ad features a before-and-after picture that is a transitional blend of the before and after photos. On the left is the original, worn-out counter. As you transition to the right, you can see what the beautiful upgraded counter looks like after Cornell was put to work. This bold photo depicts the high-end work offered and gives people a feel for the exceptional change they can get by using Cornell.

While the bottom of the ad includes a few brief bullet points, the focus is on directing clients to their website. This will allow clients to visit in the beautiful online galleries that Cornell has built up over the years. The offer at the bottom of the ad is not a coupon; rather, it is an offer to do a free photo consultation that will show what clients' kitchens and bathrooms will look like after the improvements.

As another example, David is an estate-planning attorney. While he would be drowned out in most mediums that are dominated by personal injury and social security lawyers, he feels this magazine might be a better fit. A half-page ad is plenty for him to convey his message. David includes a picture of a happy family in front of a nice home. This warm picture will create an affinity for his service and will transition readers into checking out his related storyline. Instead of boasting his credentials, he sets out to sell people on the importance of estate planning. He makes points about protecting your family and your assets and lets readers draw their own conclusions about calling him.

A popular offer for any professional is a free consultation, and David offers one for new clients to learn more about estate planning. This ad was built with a warm feel and without an aggressive attempt at closing business. David knows that people need to build a lot of trust in their attorney before they turn over their estate-planning needs.

Coupon Publications

Consumers tend to flip through these ads quickly, so make sure your ad is simple and to the point. The offer can be the focal point of the ad if it's strong enough, and you can keep the content in an easy-to-digest form. People are looking through these publications for offers in the first place, so you have to give them what they're looking for.

For example, Peter owns a Greek takeout/dine-in restaurant. They offer good family dining at a reasonable rate. Peter has always had success with coupons, and he plans to make these the focus of his advertisement. The upper half of his ad focuses on pictures of Greek cuisine in order to draw people in and consider a somewhat unique meal. In the middle, there is a mini menu with some of the popular platters and appetizers priced out.

The bottom of his ad has five different coupons. Three are for Sunday through Thursday, as those are his lighter business days. One is a buy-one-get-one-free offer on appetizers. The second is a buy-one-meal-get-one-half-off coupon, and the third is for $5 off any order of more than $20. These varying offers will give people options. The last two coupons are for dine in. One is for a free beverage with any purchase, and another is for $3 the customer's bill at any time. These coupons can even be used during the busy weekend hours.

The main reason why people hold onto coupon publications is for the restaurant ads. Most people eat out or order food at some point during the week, so these coupons work well for restaurants. Peter doesn't bog people down with facts about his restaurant. They want deals, and they don't need to be overly sold on the product.

As another example, Barrington Fence wants to get a jump on the spring season with some solid call-to-action offers. They elect to take out a full-page ad with some strong spring offers. The ad is built around three photos that not only draw consumers in, but that also display some of their options. One picture is of a chain fence, another is wood, and one is of an ornate gate. These pictures draw people in, but they also display options without using words. The ad also includes a few short blurbs about quick turnaround and professional installation.

The bottom three coupons contain aggressive offers. One is for $300 off any full installation. Another is for a free upgrade to a high-end gate. The final offer is for a free mailbox or tree with any installation. These three offers cover the gamut for offer types— money off, upgrade, and free—a great combination of offers to meet the needs of any of Barrington's potential consumers.

Direct Mail

Direct mail is similar to coupon publications except you get (and pay for) more exclusive attention from consumers. The offer is still the focal point, but you will have a slightly more engaged audience. Some people immediately throw away direct mail, but those who take the time to look are usually willing to listen to your brief pitch. Make an offer and back up its value with content.

For example, Serenity Senior Living offers assisted living to seniors who want a combination of freedom and as-needed assistance. Their goal is to reach seniors who are thinking about leaving their homes and moving into a community such as theirs. Using demographic-based direct mail, Serenity targeted home-owners over the age of 70.

The mailing has testimonials from people currently residing at Serenity. It includes a schedule of activities as well as information about available assistance. At the end of their piece, Serenity makes an offer for a free gift with attendance at an open house. This gives their potential customers extra incentive to check out the community while Serenity has an opportunity to make their sales pitch.

As another example, Murray's Tutoring specializes in preparing students for standardized testing. Using demographics, they target medium- to high-income households with children ages 12 to 17 living at home. (Yes, you can get that specific.)

Murray's Tutoring gives examples of their past students' score improvements and a brief outline of their tutoring process. At the end of the ad, they make an offer of a full refund if a child's standardized test scores do not improve. It's a very bold but realistic offer that gives a "can't lose" sense to any of their potential clients.

Billboards

Billboards work best as a branding device, so keep it simple. Use a quick line about your business or make an easy-to-remember offer to the traffic and pedestrians. If you try to stuff a billboard with content and bullet points, people won't even bother looking. If it's easy to ingest, they will. Bold pictures similar to ones found in magazines can work well, but just remember that you're working with a very limited amount of time to get your message across.

For example, Thompson & Thompson is one of the top personal injury law firms in town. They decide to purchase a billboard in one of the highest traffic locations, near a highway interchange in the city. Having previously secured a very memorable phone number, they decide to brand it in all of their advertising.

Their billboard simply reads, "Thompson & Thompson—Hurt? 555-5555." This may not seem creative, but it is a profoundly simple branding piece. Their name, who they help, and their memorable number will work better than any billboard loaded down with bullet points.

Thompson & Thompson ran their first billboard for a year and were happy with its success. In an attempt to keep it fresh, they purchased a dozen street-level billboards. Individually they have a much smaller reach, but as a whole, the mix gets a similar number of views as their first program.

Similar to their original ad, they keep things simple with a slight variation in each sign. "Thompson & Thompson—Hurt in a Car? 555-5555." Each sign changes the middle message slightly.

Also, each ad depicts a picture of the circumstance. This one obviously shows a wrecked car. The one that reads, "Hurt on the job?" may show a ladder tipping with someone on it. "Slip and fall?" might show someone on ice or water losing his footing, and so on.

Television

Keep your business name on the screen at all times. As I said before, it may seem awkward, but you must get the most out of your advertising investment.

For example, Tully's Used Cars wants to run a television ad to get more competitive. They offer a wide range of cars and want to emphasize this to the community. They put together an effective schedule with their sales representative, with plans to update footage every few weeks to update their inventory examples. The content of the commercial will remain relatively the same throughout its run.

At the bottom of the screen is "Tully's Used Cars: Routes 10 & 31" throughout the duration of the commercial. This keeps the branding intact and makes their location easy to remember.

Their goal is to make it clear that they have a huge inventory and a wide range of choices. Whomever they choose to emcee the commercial should start off touting a high-end car—even if it's out of most people's price range—just to give the maximum budget spread. They can work their way quickly through two reasonable cars and then finish with one that's less than $2,000. "We'll even sell you a winter rat or a fixer-upper if that's what you want!" Because most used-car dealerships won't even deal in autos below that price point, they will reach a much larger audience and potentially get people financed who initially come in for a low-end car.

If they're spending enough, the commercial production team should come back every two to three weeks to record the same type of commercial with new inventory.

As another example, Remy Furniture decides to take on a television campaign. They offer a range of furniture, but they want to do something memorable to make their commercial stick out while still branding their business.

Remy keeps their business name and location on the bottom of the screen for the duration of the commercial. A seemingly normal commercial kicks off in their enormous store. People get a feel for the range offered as the emcee rattles off brand names. The emcee then announces Remy's half-off weekend sale as the sound of a chainsaw takes over the commercial. "What are you doing?!" The camera pans to a man with a chainsaw cutting a beautiful sofa in half, with stuffing flying everywhere. "Just getting ready for the half-off sale!"

Of course, this is a corny little commercial, but everyone will remember the goofy bit. They could even leave the demolished sofa in the store for people to have another good laugh upon arrival.

Radio

Pay attention to what station your commercial is airing on. If it's talk radio, you're safe sticking to dialogue. If you're on a music station, try to incorporate music or vivid sounds to keep listeners tuned in. When people go from music immediately to being lectured by a commercial, they tend to tune out or even change the station.

For example, Curtis Clothing is having their semiannual clearance sale. They decide to use the radio as a way of announcing the event. They cater to a younger, urban crowd, so they decide to run spots on a hip-hop station and a top-40 pop channel. They've gotten one of the more popular DJs to do the voiceover for their commercial, taking advantage of the automatic affinity the listeners have for the station. Very straightforward, he announces when the sale is and how it's for half off everything. He names brand after brand, stating "Half off!" each time. The commercial closes with the DJ reiterating the sale date and including easy directions to the store: "Exit two, straight into Tom's Shopping Plaza."

While the commercial is running, a faint hip-hop beat in the background keeps the commercial flowing and listeners engaged. They've been listening to music for a while, so the last thing Curtis Clothing wants to do is turn them off with pure dictation.

As another example, Spike's Bikes wants to market their motorcycles to a slightly older male demographic. They elect to advertise on a sports-talk AM station. They want to inspire first-time riders to come in and learn more about purchasing a motorcycle.

The deep sound of a motorcycle engine leads in the commercial. It catches the listener off guard, as they've been listening to conversations or a sporting event. "Ever thought of owning a bike? The freedom of the open road? Come on down to Spike's Bikes, where we're offering a free motorcycle licensing class with the purchase of any bike!" This is an extremely straightforward commercial with a bold offer. It catches the listener off guard, asks a question, and then provides an idea for people who've had their interest piqued. The bold offer is unique, and it is certainly a call to action.

Social Networking

Content is almost an inapplicable consideration for social networking, but you still have an opportunity to create an image. There is no real location at which to include content, because the purpose of these sites is simply to make and build connections. So, treat online resources and real-life networking as a sort of gentle and soft approach to soliciting business. Remind people that you're out there, but don't make offers. Keep a positive image in front of your contacts, and they'll remember you when they need your business or service.

For example, Michele is a relatively new real estate agent. She uses online social media as a way to share her journey with her friends, family, and colleagues. Without directly soliciting them, she starts to brand herself to her social community as an active real estate agent. "Just landed a beautiful property on the east side with an enormous backyard!" Without saying, "Hey, do you want to buy this house?" Michele is able to put the idea into her contacts' heads. They'll get in touch with her if they're interested, without feeling as if she's soliciting everyone she knows.

"I just helped my old college friend Dena buy her first house! I'm so happy for her!" This statement shows Michele's success as a buyer's agent. Similar to the previous example, she is touting her work skills without using direct solicitation. Things like this work much better on social networking media than saying, "Wanna buy a house?"

As another example, John is a financial advisor, and he wants to attend a local mixer being thrown by the Chamber of Commerce. He packs up his business cards and heads to the event. Although some people are standing in corners or keeping to their own cliques, John is quick to introduce himself. Instead of walking up and giving his spiel, he engages people by learning more about them. By asking what they do and showing a general interest in their business or profession, he sets them up as a warm lead who, nine times out of ten, will ask the same questions back. Without seeming pushy, John begins to build a network of warm leads.

Later on, John can get in touch with these other professionals to see whether they may be a fit for any of his financial solutions. Simply because of a five-minute conversation, he will have a much better success rate than he would from cold calling.

Online Advertising

Considering you have a fraction of a second to catch the wandering online eye, make sure your ad is a link backed up with five or fewer powerful words: "$10 off at Franco's!" or "Labor Day Sale at Claire's Clothing." Give people a local name they're already familiar with and a bold offer. Make sure your website is complete, because once they click through, they're willing to give you some time.

For example, Barry owns a bar and grill near a local baseball stadium. He decides to run an ad on the team's website to entice fans to visit him after games. The banner ad simply reads, "Use your ticket stub for a free basket of fries at Barry's after any home game!" Without even clicking through the ad, people become aware of the offer. If they do choose to click his link, they'll have a chance to see what his bar has to offer. If he has more room on the ad, or if he wanted to take out another, he could announce, "Twenty-five cent wings during every away game!" Barry just doubled up on his advertising effectiveness.

As another example, a popular weather website lets people buy banner ads based on the location in which people are checking weather. Joe's Sporting Goods decides to take out an ad through this site. They've deduced that people concerned with the weather may have more of a desire to be active outdoors. "Click here for 15 percent off your next purchase at Joe's Sporting Goods!" It's a very simple and straightforward offer with an intelligent plan for targeting the demographic.

Joe could arrange for the click through to take his web viewers to his main page to entice them to look at his product lines before clicking through another link to get the coupon. Not only is Joe using a call-to-action tactic, he's driving usage on his website and getting people to spend time looking at his products.

Signage

Signs on your trucks, building, and worksites are intended for basic branding, so don't try to overload the consumer with information. Name and number should suffice, but a quick tagline can't hurt if you've got a good one. You're not trying to convey a message with signage; rather, you seek to show off your business as an active part of the community.

For example, Nate owns a printing company that serves all kinds of businesses in the area. He is clearly the top guy in town, but he knows he could benefit from a little extra branding. Tagging his delivery trucks will help him keep his name quite literally visible throughout the community. "Nate's Printing—On Time Every Time." It's a very simple statement, but it's enough to brand his company.

As another example, Carla owns a landscaping company. For years she has been working wonders for her clientele, but she finally realized it was time to come up with some signage for her work sites. Knowing that most of her clients wouldn't want a sign sticking out of the middle of their freshly landscaped yard, she came up with a slightly different approach.

One week before she was to start work on a yard, she posted a sign saying, "Stay tuned to see what Carla's Landscaping can do for *your* home!" Day by day, people in the neighborhood saw the sign and were curious to see what it was all about. A few days after it was posted, the neighbors saw her crews go to work. Carla created a sense of anticipation in the neighborhood. When the yard was complete she removed her signage, but the neighborhood certainly knew who performed the quality work.

Action Plan

Now that you've decided what mediums you'll be using, figure out what the common content will be across your marketing program.

✓ Decide what the strongest offers you can make are.

✓ Determine what images you'll use to represent your business.

✓ Identify your taglines.

✓ Work with the creative teams from each medium you've selected. If you are presented with a particularly favorable ad, advise the other mediums to alter the content and design of their ads to match the piece of your choice.

Chapter 8

Tracking and Follow-Up Marketing

- Tracking
- Remote Call Forwarding
- Coupons and Offers
- Customer Query
- Click Throughs and Impressions
- Applying Call Results
- Continued Tracking
- Evolution of Mediums
- Manning the Phones
- Answering Services
- Follow-Up Marketing
- Action Plan

You've implemented your marketing strategy. Business is better. More calls and more customers mean more money for you and your company. Sometime down the road, your sales reps come back to see how your advertising has worked out. The Yellow Pages rep asks you how many calls you've gotten.

"Well ..."

Your radio rep wants to know whether the commercials have created a buzz.

"Um ..."

The local coupon magazine wants to know whether you want to renew.

"Let me think ..."

The newspaper is running a special and wants to know whether you're ready to upgrade your ad program.

"..."

You've implemented a seemingly good marketing strategy, and business is good. Or maybe business is not good. You're not getting the results you wanted, but you don't know who has come up short.

Tracking your advertising is the number-one way to make sure you're getting the most out of the investment you're making into your own company's growth. If you can at least attempt to quantify your results, you'll be ready to make decisions down the road. How can you grow, shrink, add, and subtract advertising programs that have worked or failed for your business?

Tracking

Tracking your advertising effectiveness can be difficult, especially if you try to quantify branding results. Some companies offer specific ways to track your results, while others leave it up to you.

Remote Call Forwarding

Remote call forwarding (RCF) is a popular way to track the results of print publications. You are offered a specific phone number that will only appear in the advertisement being tracked. Your phone number may be 555-5555, but in your Yellow Pages ad, it's 555-4444. Anyone who finds you in the Yellow Pages will call the 4444 number, but they will be directly connected to your original 5555 number. Because the consumers are calling the exclusive number in the Yellow Pages, the phone company is able to track exactly how many people pick up the phone book, look at your ad, and place a call to your business.

Pros

This is a very precise way to quantify how many calls you're getting from any kind of advertisement. You can place the ad anywhere and know exactly how many times you were called from that specific marketing piece. It's a great way to do apples-to-apples comparisons between publications. If there are two big magazines in your town, you could run the same ad in both publications, each with its own special RCF number, and see which magazine out-pulls the other.

> Remote call forwarding lets you track *exactly* how many calls you get as the result of a particular ad.

Cons

If you're trying to brand your number and have people remember it, this is not the tracking method for you. There will be multiple numbers for your business floating around and no chance of it being committed to memory. If you let the advertising company set up the RCF number, they can also take it down. If you're late on a bill or decide to cancel the program, they will likely shut that number off, and you will miss out on any further calls you may have received.

RCF numbers can also do a disservice to supporting mediums. If you run an effective billboard program, people are likely still going to have to find your number elsewhere. When the consumer goes online and calls you from a number they found in an online directory, you'll credit the online directory with the RCF for the call, rather than the billboard that swayed the consumer in the first place.

What Works?

Do it yourself! If you're new to a particular medium, specifically print ads, secure the extra phone number yourself. Even though the advertising company may offer to pay for the number, you *must* do it on your own. If the ad company has the slightest reason to turn off your number, they will—so make sure *you* have the control. Once you've proven the effectiveness of a program to yourself, feel free to revert to your original number within your continued ad program—just be sure to keep the other line active for as long as you're getting calls. You might set up an RCF in a phone book that's still getting used three years down the road.

Coupons and Offers

By making offers or having coupons in your ads, you can track the results of a variety of mediums. If a customer walks in or calls with a specific coupon, you know where the customer found you.

Pros

Not only do coupons and offers help you track where customers are coming from, they also present that ever-powerful call to action to get you results. Coupons can be coded so you can see what specific mailings, location, date, and so on the call came in from. In non-print ads, you can encourage your customers to "mention this ad to receive ...," so that when they call in or visit, they directly reference the commercial or ad that swayed them.

Cons

When you're considering effectiveness, you may miss counting the people who do not bring in or reference offers. Also, in addition to paying for the advertisements containing the coupons and offers, you have to pay for or take a hit on whatever offer you're presenting. And relying on response to offers to track creative advertising will make their branding effectiveness seem weak. Although a radio ad may be branding your business, people may not always act on your offer immediately.

What Works?

Using coupons and making offers creates a double-win situation for you. You can get people through the door and loosely track the effectiveness for various mediums. Consider any strong offers you are willing to make and present them to the public. Just make sure you still have enough of a profit margin or return rate to ensure financial growth for your business. Also, make offers on simple or repetitive deals if you feel they can lead to upsells and continued business.

Customer Query

If you don't know where a customer came from, ask! Once you've established a rapport with your new customer, simply ask how he or she found out about your business. It's not an invasive personal question, and most people will understand if you simply tell them you like to track your advertising and word-of-mouth business.

If you don't know how a customer came to you, a simple query will give you the answer! Most people are happy to tell you how they heard about your company.

Pros

It's a simple and straightforward way of tracking your entire marketing strategy. You can also use the line of questioning to uncover more information about your potential customer. If you have multiple mediums working for you in your local market, you can find out which ones are resonating most with your clientele. When you find out about word-of-mouth business, you can reward and directly re-solicit the people who brought this customer to your steps.

Cons

Customers don't always know exactly where or how they found out about your business. They may have driven by your billboard 180 times in the past month, but they may not make a single mention of it when you present your questioning. Customers also do not differentiate between competing mediums. You may run an ad in two different coupon mailers, but they may not realize there are two different companies sending them publications.

What Works?

Ask away. Ask early. Because it is so important to track your results, any additional information will help. You'll want to ask as early as possible because it's also important to track what mediums you are converting the most customers from. You might get a lot of walk-in traffic from your television commercial, but you might learn that people who saw your newspaper ad have a higher propensity to buy.

Always ask the basics, but take it a little further with any customers who you feel will divulge more information. After posing the broad question, "Where did you hear about us?" start getting specific and ask things like, "Have you seen our billboards? Did you see our trucks on the road? Have you ever received anything in the mail from us?" Directly question them about any active forms of advertising you have for the public to see. Be sure to ask the general question first. If you present the specifics first, it may coach them into saying, "Yeah, it *was* that radio commercial that brought me in."

Click Throughs and Impressions

Any time you advertise online, you should be given the results of your program in the form of click throughs and impressions. Click-through numbers inform you of how many people physically click on your ad and view your website or link. Impressions refers to how many times people see your ad but do not necessarily click it.

Pros

Click throughs are the most efficient form of tracking in the history of advertising. You are able to get factual numbers (assuming you're with a legitimate website) that tell you exactly how many people were actively engaged in your ad. Impressions are a little less cut and dried because they only tell you the number of times people viewed the page on which your ad appears.

These numbers deliver more accuracy than most other mediums can provide. Impressions are especially important when you are branding your company or your offer is not contingent on a click. If you're just announcing a holiday weekend sale, people don't need to click through to become aware of your offer.

Cons

A person clicking through your ad is no guarantee that you'll get any kind of business. Because people surfing the Net are usually casually traveling from one place to another, the odds of click throughs becoming a sale are relatively slim. Also, they mean nothing if you have a poor website. Even with a solid number of clicks, without supplementary tracking, it's difficult to track how many of your customers make buying decisions.

Impressions may be high, but there is no guarantee of how many people are looking at your advertisement. If it's farther down on the screen, it may not be viewed at all unless someone is scrolling to the bottom of the page. The people selling you these ads will tout their impressions more than any other number, but that does not guarantee a high click-through percentage.

What Works?

When you're querying your customers, make sure you ask about their usage of your website and whether they've seen any of your online ads. Even with the click-through numbers, it's tough to be certain of how many are converted into a sale. Make sure you divide your investment by the number of clicks you're getting to figure out how much you're paying to drive each person to your site. If you've signed up for a pay-per-click program, you can fix that number to a set value. Generally speaking, you'll pay less for a regular banner ad, but pay-per-click gives you more control.

Applying Call Results

It may go without saying, but you can use these results to determine what works best for your business and what you can do away with. Not every medium will work for every business. And some mediums you'll want to make an even deeper investment in.

Successes

If you've had successes with a particular medium, it makes sense to continue on a similar program. It would also make sense to see whether there are any further opportunities to get more calls. If a coupon mailer worked well for you in one of their zones, why not add a few more? If you got several calls from an online directory, maybe you could get more by improving your position. Remember to let common sense govern these results. If you got a lot of calls from the Yellow Pages but you already have the largest ad in your heading, it doesn't make a lot of sense to go even larger.

Failures

If a medium hasn't delivered the results you want and you've given it a fair shake, it's best to cut it out of your marketing strategy.

If a certain medium has failed to meet your expectations, it makes sense to cut it out of your marketing strategy. Just be sure you've given it a full shot at success. Were your offers strong enough? Did you commit for a long enough time to build your brand? Was your ad competitive enough considering your competition?

Chances are, if a direction you take with your advertising doesn't work, you won't be headed there again anytime soon. That is why it's extremely important that you investigate all aspects of why your program may not have worked. Your sales rep will be sure to give you dozens of excuses, but use some of your common sense and knowledge from this book when considering why something may have failed. If you truly ran your course with that medium, cut it out completely. Don't ever feel emotionally obligated to stick with a failing program because you liked your sales rep or you want to do the bare minimum just to help out. Your disappointed customers don't come back for a little of your business just to help you out....

Continued Tracking

Although you may find success with different mediums and feel comfortable easing up on your tracking, it's still important to revisit these methods from time to time. Markets change. Consumers' buying habits evolve. Also, the medium you are with may change something about their product or its delivery.

It's a good idea to track your advertisements on a rotating monthly basis.

When you're in a comfortable position with an effective marketing strategy, consider tracking your advertisements on a rotating monthly basis. Tracking this way will allow you to keep tabs on your advertisements without spending too much time overanalyzing an already proven source of clients.

There is also a chance your ad may become stale. People can get so used to seeing the same thing that they completely pass over it. Although branding is based on consistency, a slight change here and there will keep your potential customers attentive. If you're running a print ad on a consistent basis, try changing the photo each month to keep things fresh. Record a few versions of a similar radio or television ad so that people do not see and hear the exact same thing every time. Even if the script is virtually the same, people will be more engaged with a slight change here and there.

Evolution of Mediums

It is important for you to be abreast of any changes in the production or distribution of your advertisements. Asking your sales rep for supporting circulation numbers, ratings, and so on will help you stay on top of the effectiveness of your advertising.

TV ratings and radio listenership ebbs and flows. Keep abreast of such changes to make sure you're getting the most for your advertising dollar in these mediums.

Television ratings change far more frequently than your sales rep will likely let on. As a casual viewer, you know shows may come and go. Some rise in popularity, whereas others fade out. While television deals with the ebb and flow of viewership, so will the reach of your commercial. Have your sales rep continually update your program's reach number as the new ratings come in. This is especially important if you are running a large cable campaign. With so many changes in programming and already volatile ratings, it's crucial to be updated frequently on your numbers.

Radio is subject to similar listenership changes as television, but it happens on a less frequent basis. If your local station is losing or gaining a nationally syndicated host, expect to see a change in your program's effectiveness. Pay attention to changes in local talent as well. DJs and hosts often switch stations or move on to other markets.

Newspapers are losing readership on a regular basis. Many are doing everything they can to combat the hemorrhaging of subscriptions, but be sure to get a regular account of their readership and distribution. If your salesperson ever attempts to raise the prices, make sure they are able to qualify it.

Magazine distribution changes as paid and unpaid subscriptions change. They are as easy to track as newspapers, but local magazines aren't trending downward. Pay attention to the changing themes within the magazine to make sure they are still delivering a message you want to be associated with.

Coupon magazines sometimes change their distribution numbers based on cutting out certain demographics or even ZIP codes. Stay on top of these changes, as some of these losses may be from your customer base. Also pay attention to the size of the magazine. Although growth is great, you will certainly suffer a loss if more of your competition appears in the publication or if you get buried by other advertisers.

Direct mail is usually the most static medium you'll deal with. You're always sending a fixed number of mailers, so it's up to you to make any kind of serious changes. If you're mailing a set ZIP code, be sure you're paying per home as opposed to a flat rate;

otherwise, you'll end up paying more per home in the long run. Trust me, if more addresses get *added* to your mailing, your sales rep will come calling for an investment increase.

The Yellow Pages tracks their distribution, but make sure you're aware of any re-scoping they may do from book to book. Re-scoping is when the publication changes the map of neighborhoods distributed to. There may be a small suburb to the north of your city that gets cut from the distribution, for example. If this area was important to your marketing strategy, you may need to rethink your investment or change the directory in which you are advertising.

If you sign up for a pay-per-click program online, your costs will always reflect proven usage. However, if you have a banner at a fixed rate or an advertisement in a directory, make sure you're requesting the site's hits and your impressions and click throughs each month. Just like any other medium, the popularity of websites can change for a variety of reasons.

Billboards are the most difficult medium to track for both the companies producing these ads and the businesses purchasing them. If traffic patterns change, it will take a long time for their data to be updated. Use common sense: Don't let them give you an ad that's displayed by an overpass or a bridge that is going to be closed for construction for a considerable amount of time. Billboards near sporting venues should pass on price discounts to you in the off-season, because the traffic will go way down. Check on your own billboards from time to time, just to be sure their visibility is not being compromised by any set of circumstances.

Manning the Phones

I've spent a lot of time in this book being your marketing advocate. I've even had some serious words for advertising sales reps with your best interests in mind. Unfortunately, it's time for me to turn the tables....

ANSWER YOUR PHONES!

RETURN CALLS PROMPTLY!

You can spend thousands upon thousands of dollars on the most highly tuned marketing program available to companies in your area, but if you don't answer your phones, you might as well invest that money in chocolate-flavored lampshades. You are paying good money to get your phones to ring. The only way to capitalize on this investment is by answering these calls. If you, your receptionist, or your staff cannot take these calls, return them as soon as possible. Not later today or first thing tomorrow, but as soon as you're finished doing whatever it was that prevented the call from being answered in the first place.

When I sold advertising, some clients would say the program didn't work. These were the same people who never answered anyone's calls and never returned messages (at least to me, as a salesperson). I specifically sold Yellow Pages advertising for several years. If someone has a book open in front of them and calls your plumbing company to come fix the leak that's happening right underfoot, that person will call the next guy in the book when you don't answer. If someone is looking to get three or so competitive bids on a product or service, they're not going to wait with bated breath for you to return their call.

ANSWER YOUR PHONES!

RETURN CALLS PROMPTLY!

When I ran my family's painting business, I personally answered every call I could. If I did not, our receptionist did. If she did not, one of us would call back within 10 or 15 minutes. I have always been (and continue to be) shocked at the amount of business I secure by simply answering the phones and returning calls promptly. I go do an estimate, and homeowners and business-people alike tell me, "Well, no one answered at Painter A's, Painter B said he'd call back and I still haven't heard from him, and I left a voicemail with Painter C. Your price seems fair, so let's go ahead and just get this done." People can make several-thousand-dollar buying decisions based on basic phone etiquette.

ANSWER YOUR PHONES!

RETURN CALLS PROMPTLY!

I understand you're a busy person, and you may not have the manpower to follow these two simple rules, but if you expect to get any new business without promptly answering your calls, I know a guy who wants to start making chocolate-flavored lampshades....

Answering Services

To any of you answering-service business owners out there who picked up this book, I apologize for this section....

Answering services are a waste of money and a detriment to your business. These services are nothing more than a live answering machine. Their employees are not able to answer any of your potential customers' questions, and they generally do nothing except take contact information and promise a returned call. When these services are sold to you as a business owner, they are touted as a cheaper alternative to hiring a receptionist. In reality, most receptionists are able to answer people's questions about your business and have some sales abilities. If the cost of having a receptionist is your concern, have your business line forwarded to your cell phone or one of your primary employees so that potential clients can get immediate and effective human contact.

Answering services are often ineffective. Hire a receptionist or have customer calls forwarded to your cell phone instead of spending money on this service.

Most consumers have had enough experience calling businesses to know when they're talking to a calling service. They attempt to ask questions, and they're rolled over with, "We'll have someone call you." In my personal experience with answering services, I've had problems getting return calls. It may be the business owner's laziness, or it could be from a faulty service; but in either case, I haven't had good luck getting my calls returned.

Follow-Up Marketing

Follow-up marketing can give you one of the best returns on investment for your company. Follow-up marketing is the continual solicitation of past customers and contacts for their continued business. Repeat customers are important because they do not need to be heavily solicited to get them to return to your company if you met their needs when you first conducted

Don't neglect your potential repeat customers! Engage in follow-up marketing to secure repeat business and referrals.

business with them. Also, repeat customers are the people who are giving you referrals. A healthy balance of repeat customers, referrals, and new business will keep your company thriving.

Be sure to continue making offers to your repeat clientele. Just change some of the verbiage so that the offers are in return for their loyalty and repeat business. Feel free to offer incentives for referrals as well! People love telling their friends and family about a positive buying experience they've had, but they love it even more if it might get them a small gift certificate for coffee, for example.

Email

It's important to get customer's email addresses as early in the process as possible. You may not be tech savvy, but you'll certainly learn to be (or at least pass on the duties) when you realize how much money you can save on follow-up marketing when you secure people's email addresses.

It's gotten to the point where getting email addresses is even more crucial than getting people's residential mailing addresses. When you create forms for customers to complete, make sure their email address is the second thing they fill out, after their name. If you leave it for later in the form, they'll be more likely to skip over that field.

Use these email addresses to send a bit of information either monthly or a couple of times a year, depending on how often you conduct repeat or referral business with clients. Send them coupons or offers or just give them some product or service updates to help keep your business at the front of their mind. *Do not* send out emails more often than once per month, or else people will get sick of and potentially block your emails.

Keep your follow-up emails short and to the point. Also, keep the emails short and sweet. No one wants to look at your entire inventory each and every month. Remember, the better the offer you make within these mailings, the more likely people will be to open your email each time they receive it. Be sure to include a link to your website if it's updated, just in case they are interested in some further information.

If this kind of technology is too time consuming or difficult to take on yourself, either pass it on to one of your employees or consider a company that will manage your email list for you. Although I highly recommend you avoid paying for something you can do for free on your own, it's better than not soliciting your customers for repeat business at all. Just be sure to compare the prices to direct mail or the man hours it would take for your own employee to complete this task.

Make sure you use your website to collect email addresses. If people are on your site in the first place, they likely have an interest in your product or service. They may not be ready to make a buying decision right away, but if you solicit them at a later date via email, you may get the sale. You can also use your website to collect addresses and phone numbers, but if you require too much information, your potential customers may choose to pass.

Direct Mail

Regular direct mail is an efficient form of advertising in itself, but direct mail to your established customer base is even better. Although direct mail is far more expensive than emailing your customer base, it has a higher rate of success. Email is the new junk mail, as direct mail still has to be handled. If the person handling the mail has done business with you in the past and recognizes your name, he or she will be far more likely to see what you're offering.

Be judicious in your use of direct mailings. Don't over-send!

Remember to keep the direct mail to somewhat of a minimum, just as you would with email. If people are getting mail from you on a weekly basis, but they only need your service once per year, you're going to get a different kind of phone call. As with email, you can either manage this mailing list yourself or hire a company to do the solicitation for you. Typically, a direct-mail company can deliver higher quality at lower rates, but do-it-yourself mailings can have more of a personal touch. People are more likely to open something with a traditional stamp than something with a bulk-rate ink mark.

135

Social Networking

Suggesting people join your page on an online social-networking site is a great way to keep existing customers in the loop with your business's activities. You can announce sales, offers, and events without bombarding anyone directly with your solicitation. It can also be a fun way to update people on your business. "We hired a new researcher!" or "Thinking about expanding into the vacant lot next door ..." are quick little blurbs that people may find interesting and keep your business at the front of their mind. Just as you would with any medium, keep it to a healthy minimum. No one needs to be updated on how many customers you've had before lunch or what's on the TV in your office.

Hosting social events or customer-appreciation days is another great way to strengthen your relationship with your current customer base. A simple cookout or giveaway is always fun for existing (and new) clients. Many local sports teams will offer tickets and announcements in conjunction with paid advertising. You may be able to secure some minor-league tickets for your customers and have announcements made throughout the game, thanking them for their continued business.

Phone Calls

There's nothing wrong with a good old-fashioned phone call to check up on your customers. You can keep it simple and business related so that it doesn't come across as a sales call. An accountant could call her customers to make sure they got their refunds in a timely manner. A carpenter could call customers to make sure his work held up over the winter. A call can be for anything that shows your customer you can and would like to continue to receive their business. However, be sure to keep these to a minimum, especially if you plan on soliciting customers for any kind of specific business.

You should also remember to follow up with customers who have not made a buying decision with you. This may not apply to small-ticket business types, but if you have given anyone pricing, a quote, or an estimate, make sure you call them back within a reasonable amount of time. You don't need to follow up the next day, but if you let them go too long, they'll either put their needs on hold or be solicited more effectively by your competition!

Action Plan

Without a solid plan in place to track your advertising, you'll have no way to make educated decisions about your marketing in the future. Keep track of where your customers come from and then stay on top of them!

✓ Set up remote call forwarding numbers for any print ads you would like to track.

✓ Review your offers to make sure they're strong enough to provide trackable results.

✓ Create a customer profile sheet where you can further track your results and gain more information to better solicit customers in the future.

✓ Answer your phones!

✓ Return calls promptly!

✓ Use your customers' emails, home addresses, phone numbers, and social-networking sites to continue communication with your customer base.

✓ Consider hosting a customer-appreciation day or another social event to promote your business.

Chapter 9

Industry Specifics

- Contractors
- Restaurants
- Real Estate
- Auto Dealers
- Retailers and Grocers
- Consultants and Small Businesses Operating Nationally
- Action Plan

Certain industries can benefit more from specific marketing moves than others. Some industries are so unique or so popular that they could (and do) have entire books written on marketing strategies just for their business types alone. Regardless of your industry, read each section of this chapter. You may find ideas you've never considered, and your company may be a hybrid of two or more of these business types. Each section is followed by a case study with some industry-specific recommendations.

Contractors

Builders, painters, roofers, plumbers, electricians, and so on can all benefit from similar marketing strategy moves. As a painting contractor, I have the most specific experience in this line of work with regard to marketing. In fact, some of my biases or preferences may have shown through in earlier chapters.

Home-improvement purchases are usually big-ticket items, so offering a coupon for your services is a good way to get your foot in the door.

I'm a huge fan of coupon publications for any kind of contractor. These mailings go directly into the homes you're vying to work in. Home-improvement purchases tend to be big-ticket items, so people are eager to do business with a company offering a set dollar value off for their services. No matter what your offer is, you can use it to get in the door and build a name for yourself with your new clientele. You'll also have the opportunity to up-sell, as most contractors have multiple lines of revenue. You may offer a discount on roofing that gets you in the door, only to find out the consumer is also thinking about re-siding his or her house.

Direct mail can have a similar targeted effect for a larger investment. A foundation contractor may benefit from a direct mailing that targets homes over a certain age. A good direct-mail provider could give you the ability to directly market to anyone with a home built before, say, 1940, which may make up the bulk of your business.

Branding is particularly important for home-improvement contractors.

It's important for home-improvement contractors to find at least one solid branding medium. There are a lot of trust issues between contractors and consumers. This is why referrals are so strong within this industry. No one wants to hire a kitchen remodeler who took three months and went way over budget. People will ask around when making decisions like this because they don't want to get burned. A strong branding campaign can give the public a sense of security in your company by making it seem visible and trustworthy.

If two remodelers give prices to convert someone's unfinished basement, the homeowner has a lot to consider. Suppose Al the contractor gave an estimate for $8,000, and Buck the contractor gave one for $12,000. Both estimates seem to contain the same basic steps and procedures, but one clearly costs more. Buck has been running television ads on a local station for almost a year now. Al was just someone the homeowner chose from the Yellow Pages who was quick to answer his phone. Without any recommendations from family or friends, this homeowner may feel safer doing business with Buck, even with the added cost. He seems to have a public image, whereas the homeowner had never heard about Al's services until he showed up. A good branding program helps Buck shape the way consumers think about his business, which allows him to secure this job even at a higher rate.

Case Study 1

Name: Cole's Siding

Business Type: Vinyl siding installations

Years in Business: 12

Gross Revenue: $1,200,000

Employees: 10

Cole has been serving the community for more than a decade and has build up a good referral base. He managed to generate enough sales to stay in business through word of mouth, signs, truck signs, and a listing in the Yellow Pages. He is aware that there is room for growth and is ready to update his marketing strategies. Cole also has some cutting-edge vinyl siding that is built to look like shingles. It's a very expensive product, but there has been demand in other markets where it's been introduced.

Cole gets into a coupon mailer with the maximum distribution for his area. After getting competitive bids from the three local coupon magazines, he chooses the cheapest one, which covers the same area as the other two companies. A beautiful before-and-after picture will catch people's eyes. The body of the ad outlines some simple benefits and provides information on how much siding can save homeowners in the long run. If Cole's area has any grants available for people looking to improve their energy efficiency, he should include this information in the body as well.

His three coupons have varying offer types. The first one offers $600 off any full installation. The second gives customers free window casings for up to 12 windows with any installation. The third is an offer for an upgrade to one of his more premium brands of siding—which Cole has made sure his margin will allow.

Cole has a presence in the Yellow Pages, but it could use a little attention. He runs several in-column ads under varying headings, such as General Contractors, Siding, and Home Improvements. These ads simply say, "All Ranges of Vinyl Siding to Meet Your Budget and Quality Needs." Providing number of years in business and declaring insurance coverage would also be a plus for these ads. There are two competitive directories in his town, and Cole decides to go with both because they seem to have split usage.

Cole should sit down with salespeople from radio and television stations, a billboard company, and a cable television provider. When he can pinpoint which of these can offer him the best bang for his buck, he should commit to one for his branding needs. In this case, let's assume that the cable representative was able to meet his needs better than anyone else.

His sales rep finds that a few news stations and some history and geography channels pull the best numbers. It would be wisest for Cole to go with a straightforward ad to brand his big-ticket service. With his company name and number scrolling along the bottom of the ad, he could show in slideshow form each step of the installation process and finish the ad with a testimonial from a satisfied customer. He should record several testimonials and use testimonials from the demographic that each station represents.

To move his high-end product, Cole should run a direct-mail piece based on the top percentage of home values in his area, totaling around 2,500 homes. This piece should take advantage of any marketing images his supplier can provide. The content should review the energy benefits that come from upgrading to vinyl, describe the maintenance savings over the long term, and include persuasive materials explaining why this is the finest siding available.

Cole should run a 2,500-address mailing again the following month, but this time he should select the top percentage of income in his community to total that number. It's a good idea for him to rotate his mailing, because the wealthiest people do not always live in the most expensive homes, and people living in expensive homes do not always have a high income posted. People with substantial assets do not always post the highest income. Retired people and business owners do not have their wealth reported in the same way, depending on how they file taxes, earn their income, and so on.

Somehow, Cole has gotten away without a website for the past 12 years. Cole should put word out that he's in need of website design and take advantage of a small local provider who can give him personal attention at a reasonable rate. When the site is up and running, he should contact his two Yellow Pages sales reps to have his site linked on their directories.

As a contractor, it's important for Cole to make sure he is visible when people are looking for siding or specifically for his business. This is taken care of through his online and Yellow Pages programs. A bit of branding through his cable ads will keep his name at the front of people's minds if they are considering siding. The coupon mailer will keep him in front of the masses with aggressive offers to bring in his bread-and-butter clientele. The direct mailing to high-end consumers will serve as an outlet for his new vinyl shingle siding.

Restaurants

Restaurants are another type of business that I could spend a hundred more pages talking about. Continued and consistent marketing is crucial for any type of restaurant. Even long-standing establishments need to make some marketing moves to keep their loyal customers coming back. I will break restaurants up into three categories for the purposes of discussion: takeout, family dining, and fine dining.

Continued marketing is crucial even for long-established restaurants.

Takeout

Takeout restaurants can be anything from pizza and sub shops to Chinese or fish-and-chips joints. Most of these establishments survive on volume and frequent repeat business. Some of their customers come in several times per week or even daily.

Number-one rule for a takeout restaurant's marketing strategy? Get your menu out there!

The single most important marketing move for any business of this type is getting your menus in front of your consumer base. This makes it easier for people to become familiar with your offerings, place their orders much faster, and even phone in their orders for pickup or delivery. It's also important for these menus to contain dated coupons to encourage a return visit as soon as possible. When people are making these lower-ticket purchases, it's okay to make relatively simple offers. You're not trying to inspire new customers as much as you're trying to keep your current customers hooked.

Be sure to give out menus each and every time someone places an order. If you have drivers, keep them stocked so they can leave menus behind in apartment buildings, hotel/motels, offices, and so on. Make sure you mail out or hand-deliver menus to everyone within a one- or two-mile radius of your business. You may be right under their noses, but they'll need your menu and offer to make continued purchases at your restaurant. Even established chains need to get their menu out as often as possible.

Creative advertising can be difficult for businesses that already have a limited profit margin. For example, a stand-alone location may have a hard time sustaining an effective television or radio program. Also, these mediums reach a very wide audience, whereas your restaurant likely only serves customers within a small radius. However, anyone with a local chain might want to consider these venues, as they would have enough locations to cover a regional advertising campaign.

Case Study 2

Name: Lee's Chinese Takeout

Business Type: Chinese food takeout and delivery

Years in Business: 4

Gross Revenue: $350,000

Employees: 5

Lee runs a Chinese takeout restaurant that has managed to stay afloat past the new-business hump of four years. Lee's good location has led to most of his new business, and his quality food has kept his customers coming back. Other than the menus Lee has had printed out, the only other marketing he has done is a grand-opening banner he had for a few months and a free business listing in the Yellow Pages. Lee is getting by, but he wants to make his business truly prosperous.

The first thing Lee should do is make some slight changes to his menu. He can keep everything as is, but he must include several coupons. It may be a tough decision for him to make, but a very slight price increase might be in his best interest to cover his marketing investment. More importantly, Lee can have a large print order for his menus that he can use for several years without worrying about inflation.

The coupons should promote larger orders. Six coupons with three price points should suffice. He could have coupons for $2 off any order more than $20, $4 off any order more than $35, and 10 percent off any order more than $50. The free offers should include two free eggrolls with any purchase more than $20, free pork fried rice with any order more than $35, and free spareribs with any order more than $50.

This range will allow people to either add more food or get a few bucks off their order—whichever is most appealing. As a rule of thumb, the free items should be valued slightly more than the dollar-value offers, as you have some profit margin built into the price of all your products.

A local newspaper allows for inserts with certain editions. Lee should sign on to the minimum run—say, 1,000 pieces—and have his menus delivered to homes within his delivery range. The newspaper can rotate the exact areas so he can cover his whole radius within a year at a reasonable rate.

Lee instructs his drivers to leave a menu with each delivery order. Also, any deliveries going to apartment buildings, businesses, hospitals, dorms, and so on should include a large number of extra menus for receptionists and common areas.

Because he has a somewhat limited budget for branding, Lee should at least get some light-up signs for his delivery drivers to place atop their vehicles.

Near his restaurant is a community center with some indoor basketball courts. Lee may be able to work out some trade to put his name out there. Perhaps Lee agrees to cater four events per year (with some limitations) in exchange for the right to hang a sponsorship banner in the basketball gym. For the price of producing a few big meals per year, he's able to brand himself with some of the local community.

Lee does not have to make too many big changes to his marketing plan to improve his overall reach. His menus are more effective, they're getting in the hands of more people, and he has a bit of branding out there without breaking the bank.

Family Dining

The best coupon offerings for family-dining restaurants are the ones that get people to dine in groups.

Family-dining restaurants include any sit-down restaurants that cater to families, business groups, couples—anyone looking for the convenience and enjoyment of dining out while keeping somewhat of a budget in mind. Most national chain restaurants (besides fast food) fall into this category.

Although customers of these kinds of restaurants are looking for reasonable prices, there is much room for up-selling and profitability if you can keep your seats full. The best kinds of coupon offerings for these restaurants are the ones that encourage people to dine with other people. "Buy one, get one half off" and "Buy one, get one free" are some great common coupons you can use to bring in multiple customers. I've even seen some good offers for "Kids eat free" or "Buy three, get one free." These offers obviously bring in complete families and larger groups.

While traditional coupon publications make sense, consider running these ads in places where you can inspire and catch people off guard. A nice newspaper ad with a strong offer might get someone to consider visiting your restaurant for the first time or even to return after a long absence. One of your prior patrons may be checking the sports section for last night's scores, only to see your ad and remember his experience with your restaurant. Instead of having meatloaf Monday, he might bring the family back to your establishment!

Creative advertising works better for family restaurants than it does for takeout places. Just be sure to include a solid offer. A billboard announcing, "Anthony's: Home of the $12.99 Rib-Eye Platter" is a good way to brand your restaurant using one of your featured dishes. You might consider a radio or television commercial aired early in the day that talks about your evening specials (happy hour, half-price appetizers, buy one get one ribs, and so on). Not only can you bring people in on a day-to-day basis, you can even start to brand your business's specials. People may eventually think without prompting, "Let's go to Patterson's tonight after work. They do half-price appetizers at the bar on Wednesdays!" Offers specific to the bar can bring in some great drink sales with large profit margins.

Case Study 3

Name: Zeke's Bar and Grill

Business Type: General American pub fare, grilled foods, and a full bar

Years in Business: 8

Gross Revenue: $1,100,000

Employees: 18

Zeke's is becoming a very popular hangout in the community. Reasonable prices, a sporty environment, and good food and drinks keep people coming back. Business is good, but Zeke pays high rent on a building that is rarely filled to capacity. Any additional income would be warmly welcomed.

Zeke has a good location, purchased a great website, and has a smaller street-level billboard farther up the main drag. His signage and Yellow Pages listings are sufficient.

The first step in improving his business should include securing his regulars. One of the smaller independent newspapers in his area is known for its calendar section of events and is popular with other restaurants. Zeke gets competitive and takes out a half-page ad. The content of this ad should include daily specials so people can grow accustomed to Zeke's offerings. I would suggest something along these lines:

Monday nights, half-priced appetizers in the bar until close.

Tuesdays, two-for-one drinks.

Wednesday night, kids eat free.

Thursday, 30-cent wings.

Friday nights, karaoke.

Saturday, game-day specials all day.

Sunday, 1/2 chicken or 1/2 ribs 1/2 off.

These day-to-day offerings will become second nature to Zeke's guests, and he will build specific clientele for each day. This includes food and drink offerings, kids' specials, and two event-themed days.

Zeke should also do some branding of these same events on a daily basis. Each day during the evening commute, Zeke should run a radio ad for the daily special. Even if it is just one spot per day, it will have a very strong branding effect in due time.

A unique way to draw in groups of diners and drinkers would be to offer a free sampler-platter appetizer for any groups of five or more wearing uniforms. Zeke could have a banner at a local softball field where many adult teams play socially. If any nearby bowling alleys allow advertisements, those would be another good place to put this offer out.

Because Zeke invested so much money in his website, he should certainly put it to good use. Using some online social networks, he can build a fan page where he announces his daily specials and offers a link to the restaurant's website. On occasion, he could offer a special coupon to anyone who signs up for his fan page.

These marketing additions will certainly help Zeke fill the vacant seats in his restaurant. He's put out great daily offers and has used them to brand his actual calls to action. The social networking and group offers are two creative and low-cost additions.

Fine Dining

Fine-dining restaurants are where people go for special occasions, dates, or just a high-end meal for people with more disposable income. Offers for these kinds of establishments must be highly camouflaged in order for them to be effective. No one wants to whip out a crinkled $10-off coupon at the end of a date (at least not early in the relationship), but it's still possible to get people hooked on your high-quality food with a roundabout offer. Use a typically slow business night to create an event based on value. You'll still stay out of the red, but you'll be able to get people in to get a taste of the good life at a better price. A beautiful ad in a high-end magazine could display one of your artful dishes in your well-decorated restaurant, but somewhere in the advertisement you should mention, "Tuesday night is McFancy's Tasting Night. We offer a three-course sampling for just $20!" or "Wednesdays at McFancy's is Wine Tasting Night! We offer 20 bottles of wine for under $20, as well as a three-glass wine flight for just $10."

Patrons of fine-dining establishments aren't likely to use a coupon, but they will often respond to carefully worded specials or events that are advertised.

These offers have been disguised as specials or events, which makes them a little more palatable for people who wouldn't be caught dead using a coupon. Of course, people on Tuesday will order drinks, and you can have add-ons or extras along with the meal to protect your bottom line. Wednesday night may bring in some winos, but winos like to eat, too.

Offers are great, but they're not the bread and butter of most fine-dining establishments. A variation on social marketing can do wonders for your business. Most cities and even towns have festivals or events that feature restaurants in the area. These are usually fee-based events often sponsored by local advertising companies, such as newspapers and radio stations. These events allow you to brand your business with food rather than just ad copy. You can tell people how great your restaurant is until you turn blue, but getting people to taste your product is the best way to get them hooked. Sign up for a booth or take part in a weekend of special offerings. However the event is being orchestrated, consider taking part.

Social marketing is an effective advertising tool for fine-dining establishments.

Online advertising also works well for high-end restaurants. When people are looking for something nice for their special event, they're more likely to take the time to check out websites, pictures, and online menus. If you really are putting out a good product, many of the online directories allow people to review businesses for free. These reviews attach themselves to your listing and can sway people (both ways) when they're considering your restaurant for the first time.

An online presence will also help you to pull in business travelers, who often have larger budgets or per diems that can be spent on quality food. They'll likely flip open their laptop and search for restaurants in your area. Be sure to make yourself available!

Online social networking is also a great way to keep your local clientele informed and coming back for more. Any real foodies will likely sign up for your page and be glad to hear about your unique daily specials. Unlike in other types of businesses, most people who sign up for your page will welcome daily updates and pictures of your newest creations.

Case Study 4

Name: Pierre's Bistro

Business Type: High-end French dining and wine bar

Years in Business: 14

Gross Revenue: 1,900,000

Employees: 18

Pierre has had great success with his bistro by providing his diners with an elegant experience and some of the finest food in town. His expansive wine list is second to none. His restaurant has been able to function on local reviews and word of mouth, but Pierre needs growth to open a second restaurant.

Pierre should get in touch with some of the magazines in his area. His goal should be to write an editorial piece or give a few recipes that could be coupled with some paid advertisement. Pierre's contributions will solidify him as a culinary expert. The ad should picture a well-dressed table for two with two of his most extravagant-looking dishes. Very simply stated, the ad could read, "An Experience Like No Other, at Pierre's French Bistro."

Without being a coupon or even a set price off, the ad could offer something like this: "New diners can come in and experience French cuisine for just $45 (includes a three-course meal for two; wine pairings extra).

This offer could change from month to month. Here are some other offers that will bring in clientele without cheapening the experience:

Come in and experience our five-course prix fixe, just $65 for two.

Tuesday nights are wine-tasting nights—a new region each week.

Five courses, five wine pairings, just $100 per couple.

Wednesday nights are tapas nights; smaller portions just $8 per plate.

Come in and try our exotic fish of the week for just $15.

These offers could rotate throughout the year. Alternating photos will also keep the ad looking fresh—a larger table, a panoramic view, and so on.

For all 14 years he's been in business, Pierre has been solicited by a local event company that holds a dining-out week in his area. For a fee and certain menu discount requirements, Pierre can be listed as a participating restaurant during this designated week. Pierre looks past his pride and signs on to give the community a chance to taste his offerings at a reduced price. This kind of event will open more people's eyes to his food without Pierre having to go too far outside of his discount comfort zone.

Pierre becomes more active with his online social marketing and begins sharing food pictures with people online. By sharing and giving people a sense of being on the inside, Pierre creates a special affinity with his customers.

Pierre managed to improve his marketing strategy without compromising his prestige.

Trade

Depending on the product or service you're offering, you may be able to pay for some of your advertising in trade.

If you own any kind of restaurant, talk to your sales rep about potentially doing some of your advertising in trade. Advertising companies are always looking for credits and gift certificates that can be used on other businesses they are soliciting or sometimes as rewards for salespeople. This is an obvious benefit to you—you do not have to come up with cash, and you end up paying a lot less when you consider the cost of the value of your gift certificates. If you pay off a $1,000 invoice with $1,000 cash, there goes $1,000 cash. If you pay it off with $1,000 in gift certificates, you only have to consider the cost of the value of those certificates. A thousand dollars worth of dining may only cost you $600 or $700, depending on your profit margin. If you own a business other than a restaurant that offers other business-to-business services, be sure to ask your sales rep whether they will accept any portion of your bill as trade.

Real Estate

Real estate is one of the wildest industries to work in. The market is constantly fluctuating, and people's buying patterns change based on market conditions. There can be quite a bit of money made in real estate, yet a very small percentage of agents bring in a primary income in this field.

Two things separate successful agents from part-time salespeople. The first is ability. Because anyone can get into real estate if they pass certain tests, anyone can take a shot. With so many people trying it out but not having what it takes, the agents who *do* know what they're doing have a chance to shine. Second, proper marketing will help good agents become multimillion-dollar salespeople. All things being equal among talented agents, the ones with the best marketing plans will come out ahead.

Agents need to focus on marketing themselves as well as the individual properties they are responsible for selling.

Self-Marketing

Agents need to bring in new buyers and sellers as often as possible in order to build their book of business. It's a common practice for a realtor to use his or her listings as a way to also secure buyers. When a potential buyer calls about a property on which they saw a sign, the agent may convince the person to sign a buyer's agreement so they can work together to find the right property. Open houses are also a great way for agents to bring in new buyers. Realtors need to focus the majority of their self-marketing on obtaining sellers, which will lead to securing buyers.

Although their needs may vary, sellers generally want an agent who will sell their property at the best price in a speedy fashion. This is the image agents need to convey to homeowners in order to secure their business.

More than in almost any other industry, realtors rely heavily on referrals for their business. Buying or selling a home is an intense life event, so people want an agent they can trust. This is also why there are a lot of part-time agents in the industry. They sell the homes of their family members and friends and are content moving just a few homes per year.

To capitalize on these relationships, realtors need to rely on their network of friends and family early on. Sending these contacts reminders and updates about the local market can help you get references when they are looking to buy or sell and when their contacts are looking to do the same.

To amplify the effects of good work and a solid network, agents must brand themselves. If they want to pick up business outside of their network, an effective branding campaign is a must.

A consistent omnipresence is crucial in marketing yourself as a real-estate agent.

People do not usually wake up one day and say, "It's time to sell the house!" It's a long, contemplative process. This makes it difficult for you to target your potential customers in a specific moment. A plumber offering emergency service must be in a phone book because it's what people pick up in a home-plumbing emergency. Realtors do not have that specified window. A consistent omnipresence is key. At the same time, most real-estate agents do not have the budget, especially early on, to flood their entire market with a grand branding scheme.

The best move is for an agent to take advantage of "warm" branding options. These are things such as church bulletins and sponsorships—anything that would market to people who already have a warm connection with your medium. People who attend a particular church usually do so in a positive fashion. These feelings tend to blend with their perception of the people advertising in the church bulletin. The same thing can be said about sponsorships. A family with youngsters on a Little League team that you sponsor subconsciously builds a warm connection with you because of your link to the organization. These mediums build positive emotions similar to the ones you have in your network of friends, family, and colleagues. When it's time to sell, you'll be one of their top-of-mind providers.

Advertorials are also an excellent way to build the community's trust in you as a real-estate agent. Some publications will allow you to write articles for them if you are a paid advertiser (and you have something of value to say). Consider an ad in a local magazine and write an article on local market trends, staging, or anything that might be of interest to your community. Your ad as it stands alone in a magazine is just a bunch of claims, a face, and a phone number. That same ad next to an informative article will be built up because of an earned respect.

Although most of your marketing should be focused on first getting listings to generate buyer leads, there is one unique avenue I would consider if I was looking to sign more buyers. People with growing families are often looking to increase their living space. Why not consider running an ad in a motherhood special a local paper is running or even sponsor a Lamaze class? These may seem like unusual avenues, but they are cost-effective ways you can build bonds with people who may be looking to make a move.

Also, if you have a college or university in your area, you could also consider marketing yourself to graduate students. There may be a school newspaper or even an on-campus billboard you could use to market yourself to these well-educated buyers. Financing may be dicey depending on their work history, but I imagine most people seeking an advanced degree may have the means to make a first-time purchase in the near future. Many of these students may also already be locally employed and furthering their education on their company's dime.

Property Marketing

Great! Now, you've got 20 properties listed and you're ready to go. However, the market is slow, and you need to do something to make sure your properties get first looks from potential home-buyers in the area. You can certainly list them in all of the data-bases and even spend some money on dropping them into the sea of houses advertised in the newspaper. But what can you do to make your property stand out? Sure, you can throw it up on a billboard for a month or two, but there goes your entire commission. Unique marketing for properties has to be closely tied to the potential buyer's habits. Many (if not most) listings will be too broad-ranging to target specific buyers, but others will be easier to define.

If you have a listing for a camp on a lake or river, why not consider a little ad in the sports section of your paper? Owning a second property is not usually a necessity, but your ad may inspire someone who's had it in the back of his mind to take a look. Selling a commercially zoned lot or building? Business own-ers are likely your top buyers, so why not run an ad in a business journal or, better yet, make some connections with your local Chamber of Commerce to create a little buzz between the mem-bers. If you've got an in with the chamber, you could take the creativity level even higher and offer to host and cater their next meeting at one of your vacant commercial properties!

For a typical residential property, it may be a little more difficult to capture specific buyers in one location, and it may also be cost prohibitive to spend a lot of your budget on marketing just one specific house. If your client is comfortable with it, you could send or hand-deliver information on the property to people within a certain radius. Most people have a vested interest in their own neighborhood, so who better to create a buzz than the neighbors? They may know people interested in their neighborhood because of their exposure to the area. They may also be considering buying or selling in the future, so it would be good for your busi-ness for them to have their eyes on your progress (assuming you do a good job).

Real estate is one of the few industries where you are simply a middleman between buyers and sellers. You have no inventory to purchase and very little overhead. It's important to treat your marketing costs like basic operating costs. You may make more money percentage-wise per sale without it, but there's no way you'll reach the numbers that top agents achieve in your market without advertising.

Case Study 5

Name: Waverly Real Estate

Business Type: A real estate team that is part of a national brand

Years in Business: 3

Gross Revenue: $90,000

Employees: 3

Waverly Real Estate is an independent team that is part of a local brokerage of a national company. Although they are able to operate as agents of a larger brand, they are treated as independent contractors responsible for their own business costs and local marketing. It's been a slow start for the Waverly team, as their marketing has been limited to property signage, free online services, and the solicitation of their personal networks.

The Waverly team begins to direct-mail the neighborhoods in which they are selling homes. They do this the old-fashioned way, by collecting addresses and stuffing envelopes. Inside there is a letter introducing the team to the neighborhood and talking about the new listing just up the street. The team takes advantage of the neighbors' assumed affinity for the area and asks them to spread the word about the available home. The neighbors may want like-minded people in the area, so they will likely speak with any of their friends or family members who are considering making a move. Also, the letter asks the recipients to keep the Waverly team in mind if they ever choose to sell their home.

This move will focus the neighborhood's attention on the property for sale. Assuming the team does good work, their reputation will gain credibility, and their properties will begin to move at a faster pace.

To brand their name and improve community relations, the Waverly team sets out to sponsor some local youth sports teams. These investments will turn the parents of the young athletes into warm leads. As long as the team makes some appearances at the sporting events or celebrations, they will be able to add many families to their database.

The Waverly team currently has two big-ticket properties listed. If they move these two units, they'll make hefty commissions and will likely draw in other similar listings.

Using a direct-mail service, the Waverly team sends some property data sheets to other homes with similar values—just a selection that may associate with people with similar buying capabilities. Who knows—they may be considering a local move themselves. Also, the team chooses to list the properties in a local business journal. This paper does not usually have listings included, but this out-of-the-box technique will put the properties in front of many qualified buyers.

By using unique branding techniques for both their business and their listings, the Waverly team can improve on their marketing without blindly spending their money on every passing opportunity. As the team grows their database, their sales and ability to increase their marketing strategy grows as well.

Auto Dealers

Most new-car dealers are intermingled with a national advertising campaign for the brand they are selling. National commercials run with local tags at the end announcing the local dealership. They also have inflated marketing budgets that are helped out by co-op dollars from the manufacturers. This section is more for used-car dealers or people with emerging dealerships who are looking for a unique branding edge.

Similar to real-estate agents, you are responsible for branding your company while also marketing vehicles on the individual level. Many dealers fall into the trap of concentrating too much on the latter aspect. If you market cars on an individual level, it's a yes or no on that particular vehicle. If the price or specifics are wrong, your potential buyer will continue looking through whatever publication you spent money listing the vehicle in. If you're lucky, the consumer may have come in to view the car, allowing you to take a shot at selling him or her a different model.

There are some places online where you can list cars for sale for free. This can be a great tool for the vehicles you are trying to sell on an individual level without spending a lot of money on something that may be passed over. It's never good to mislead any potential buyers, but if you do list on one of these sites, consider leaving out your business name. People do not always feel comfortable working with dealerships, so they may be quick to overlook a potential model if they see it branded with your dealership name. Simply list the car info with your phone number, and people will take more time to review the data.

As a used-car dealership, focus your strategy on bringing in open-minded buyers.

As stated before, focusing on individual cars should not be the focus of your marketing campaign. The reality is, if someone is looking for a specific model, they will be able to find it whether it's with your dealership or another. What you should focus your marketing strategy on is bringing in open-minded buyers. You want people who are not fixed on a specific model, a certain budget, or even special credit needs. Because every other dealership out there generally has similar credit options and a range of budgets to meet people's needs, those are *not* the things you need to focus on in your marketing strategy. These basic items should be included in some of your marketing materials, but again, they should not be the focus. In other industries, you need to compete with your competition by focusing on things that make your business unique. In the world of car sales, you're competing with the industry itself.

Because most dealerships, whether selling new or used cars, all offer the same things almost on a nationwide scale, the focus must be on differentiating yourself from the masses. These masses have also built up a reputation of being an industry no one is excited to deal with. I know there are always exceptions to the rule, and there are plenty of honest and upright salespeople out there, but our focus is on getting you more customers, not on political correctness.

For this particular marketing plan to work, it involves a little bit of business-plan compromise as well. People love silent sales. People love to be able to look through your inventory without being solicited by a salesperson. This is why having an updated website with the inventory is a must for any dealer, regardless of their size. Consumers also want to test-drive cars on their own. This may require a special type of insurance, but it's worth considering.

If I ran a used- or new-car lot, I would brand my dealership as the salesperson-free dealership. It may seem corny and gimmicky, but I would refer to my salespeople as "order takers." Of course they would still be salesmen, but if people feel there will be a very unique hands-off approach with people facilitating and not forcing a sale, you will get many more customers through the door. I would even go as far as to say, "Our order takers wait in their offices until you express that you have some questions or would like to make a purchase. No swarms of salespeople waiting for your arrival." This message could be amplified over any kind of branding medium. Radio and television commercials that depict these exact circumstances would be sufficient. Print ads can talk about offers, sales, and financing but contain a message of your unique business plan.

There's nothing wrong with the traditional marketing that has gone on for years in the auto industry, but without any level of creativity or uniqueness, the only gauge of marketing ability is who is spending the most. Tim's generic ad about financing has been seen three times by a consumer, and Bill's ad has been seen 15—so Bill gets the business. However, with a more unique approach that goes against the grain, Tim's revamped marketing and business strategy involving a hands-off approach may out-pull Bill's bloated budget.

Case Study 6

Name: Brandon's Used-Car Emporium

Business Type: Used-car sales

Years in Business: 6

Gross Revenue: $1,200,000

Employees: 4

Brandon has been selling used cars with two friends and a receptionist for the past six years. Business has been good, but he wants to compete with some of the bigger lots in his area. He has used the local paper to list some of his cars, and he has also used a few online auto classifieds.

Brandon needs to do something to set himself apart from the competition. He decides to set up his lot based on price. While most dealerships in the area group cars by type, he wants to address his customers who are shopping on a budget.

Television seems to be the best place for Brandon to convey his new sales approach. The television station records a straightforward commercial that depicts Brandon's lot and the new layout. Appearing in his own commercial, Brandon touts his company's low-pressure sales process and their budget-match guarantee, in which they will only show customers cars in their personally designated budget. If any of his salespeople tries to upsell a customer, that customer gets a free $100 gas card!

Brandon matches this bold offer with a similar offer in the local newspaper. Instead of offering a bunch of cars in the limited space he can afford, Brandon features one "car of the week" that includes a free $100 gas card with purchase. The unusual layout of the ad draws in people and helps to brand his business. Although he may only break even on the cost of the ad against the profit on the car sale, Brandon begins to create an image for his business.

Brandon elects to sponsor a youth driving course once per week. Each week, he'll pay for five students with good grades to take their required driver's education on Saturday afternoon. Brandon arranges for good rates from a local provider for the guaranteed business and uses this investment to create contacts. These students and their parents will be far more likely to consider Brandon for the car purchase that is likely on the horizon.

This car lot is poised to grow with their new marketing strategy. Brandon has set out to have a different image from the rest of the dealers in town and has created many warm connections in the process.

Retailers and Grocers

Marketing for retailers and grocers is a necessity, but it can be harder to quantify than any other industry. If you run your own coupons that can help, but because of the volume of business you're doing, it's difficult to query your clientele. Fortunately, your potential customer base is very black and white. People are either shopping price or shopping brand quality. If you have competitive prices, you need to focus your marketing on making your prices highly visible to consumers. If you're selling unique or high-quality brands, you have to make it known to the people who are looking. Your store may be doing a little bit of both, but it's important for you to treat them as separate entities.

In the retail or grocery industries, people shop either for price or for brand quality. Plan your marketing strategy accordingly.

Newspaper inserts and direct mail are a must if you're looking to get a wide range of prices out to the consumer. If you're a smaller retailer, the newspaper itself can be a good place for a smaller ad if you only need to list a few specific items. Radio ads are also a good way to update your deals to people who may not be considering making a buying decision until they're inspired by your price.

When you want to grab consumers looking for high-end or unique products, you need to slim down the range and specify the demographic. A grocer could do well in a local high-end magazine if they wanted to feature a selection of exotic mushrooms or spices that the typical consumer may not be interested in. A visually appealing commercial on a cable cooking show would also be a great way to inform the foodies about new and exotic offerings. Small retailers can benefit from the same thing. And it makes perfect sense for a shoe store to have an affordable commercial on a cable station targeting their exact demographic.

If you have enough customer access to get their email or residential addresses, it's very important to keep customers updated about your pricing and inventory. As stated earlier, retention marketing is extremely important for businesses that see their customers on a frequent basis. Most people go to the grocery store no less than once per week. And most retailers can expect to see familiar faces more often than contractors or accountants do. This is why it's important for you to stay at the top of your customers' minds. You don't want them to cut back on their visits, and you certainly don't want them heading off to your competition just because you decided not to advertise directly to them.

Case Study 7

Name: Henrique's Latin Market

Business Type: A small grocery store with a focus on Latin products

Years in Business: 4

Gross Revenue: $450,000

Employees: 11

Henrique owns a grocery store that specializes in Latin products. They have all kinds of spices, produce, and meats typically associated with Latin food. Henrique has penetrated the Latin population pretty well, but he knows more people would visit his store if they knew what they were missing.

In the past, Henrique has used a small circular that is directly mailed as an insert to a nearby neighborhood that is predominately Latino.

To bring people to his grocery store in search of relatively exotic ingredients, Henrique needs to target people with culinary curiosity. The most obvious choice of advertising medium is a cable cooking channel. The crew shoots a commercial on location, depicting the exotic offerings as well as the wide range of day-to-day products available at Henrique's Market. To call viewers to action, Henrique is willing to give a shaker's worth of a free homemade Latino spice rub to anyone who mentions the ad.

Henrique decides to continue with his circular, but he also purchases a small street-level billboard in a neighborhood with a high per-capita income. He uses stunning visuals to depict some of the most exotic foods he carries. This kind of advertisement would certainly entice people with a bit of expendable income who may want to get creative in the kitchen.

Part of Henrique's new marketing strategy includes better collection of his customers' email addresses. Using his new-and-improved database, Henrique sends out his circular in a digital fashion and includes a free recipe for a Latin dish.

By reaching out in creative and affordable ways, Henrique is able to bring in new customers and expose them to his unique grocery store. In time, his new database will allow him to cut back on the number of circulars he sends out, as many of his customers will receive them digitally.

Consultants and Small Businesses Operating Nationally

Consulting is one of the most common types of small businesses in America and is growing at a very fast rate. Similar to the way outsourcing works, businesses can save money by bringing in consultants for a fixed goal or timeframe, as opposed to hiring a full-time employee or spreading others too thin. No matter what industry someone is knowledgeable about, there is a potential market for his or her brainpower. I worked in advertising for a long time, so now I consult small businesses on marketing and advertising. Someone who worked as a school administrator for an extended period of time may be sought after by other districts to consult on various projects. Engineers are often hired on a consultative basis to help with a specific part of a larger project.

Small businesses operating on a national scale can benefit from similar marketing moves. Consultants typically solicit business on a national scale, and even the ones who work regionally still need a similar type of presence.

How do these consultants make enough connections to stay in business? Because of their tenure within their respective fields, it is possible that they have enough professional contacts to stay gainfully employed for as long as they choose. Others may need to take a more proactive approach.

A consultant's website is the most important part of his or her marketing program.

The single most important part of a marketing program for a consultant is his or her website. It's the consultant's official calling card and the very first exposure most potential clients will have to the business. Again, people judge books by their covers. If you have a professional and updated website, clients will get the feeling that you, too, are professional and are on the cutting edge of your technology. Make sure to have all of your services clearly outlined and explained. Provide past customer testimonials if you have any available, and be sure to have a good number of references available upon request. Never post your references' contact info online, or they'll stop giving you references when they get bombarded with unwanted solicitations.

To drive people to your site, you must focus on two key avenues. First, be sure to be well invested in several large search engines. To bring down the cost, focus on very specific keywords that have not already been oversaturated by larger companies with bigger budgets. If you are a consultant who helps larger companies coordinate moves, you could pay to be listed when people type "movers" into the search engine. Obviously, you would be buried in ads from residential movers and large national moving companies. Consider refining your keywords to "Corporate Moves," "Office Relocations," or "Business Moving Consultants." Also, be sure to take advantage of a free or paid listing on several directories as well.

Second, you must build a marketing package that you can mail to potential clients. Again, suppose you're a moving consultant. You could create a one-sheet marketing piece that also directs people to your website. Handpick clients that you would potentially work with and send out a mailing. If you get a warm lead from a phone solicitation, send off your mailing to a more refined number of businesses. You could also be creative and target commercial real-estate brokers. Obviously, they will be helping businesses buy, sell, and rent new locations, so if you had a few ins in some large markets, the referrals would start coming.

The basic rule of thumb for small businesses operating nationally or even internationally is to target the audience down to the most specific potential client. It can become extremely cost prohibitive to market on a wide scale when you're only looking to reach a very minute percentage of the population. Another great venue for advertising can be trade magazines. If there is a publication that your exact demographic has their hands on, it only makes sense to advertise to them. Just be sure to back it up with a strong online presence.

Case Study 8

Name: Perry's Custom Pocket Watches

Business Type: Built-to-order retro pocket watches

Years in Business: 1

Gross Revenue: $49,000

Employees: 1

Perry recently turned a hobby into an additional source of income. He custom-builds pocket watches to order. Some are novelty pieces, whereas others are a bit higher end.

All of the work Perry has done in the past year was for friends and a few referrals. His first marketing investment was a website, but now it's time to grow.

Perry learns that he can buy into a pay-per-click program on a popular search engine for just a few cents per click. When people search "pocket watches" online, they will see Perry's mini-ad leading them to his website. In the interim, Perry works to build up his online social networking page.

Perry researches where other custom jewelers do some of their national advertising. He finds a reasonably priced magazine that features other advertisers who sell customized jewelry. Having an extremely unique product to offer, Perry does not need a huge full-page spread; instead, he opts for a quarter page with a picture of one of his most ornate pocket watches and the bold title, "Customize Pocket Watches" and his website listed. Considering that there aren't many other people doing what he's doing, Perry can advertise the idea without having to focus too much on selling himself.

Twice per year, Perry signs up to attend a few jewelry conventions. These two events will help him make connections with potential buyers, but more importantly, they will put him on the map with bigger jewelers who may make purchases through him for their loyal customers.

Perry is able to do business on a national level out of his home, without spending a fortune, and he can continue to grow as large as the market will allow.

Action Plan

Understanding that your specific industry may have different marketing needs will help you to make better advertising decisions. See what similarities you can draw between your business and the examples in this chapter.

✓ Determine whether your business falls into any of these industries.

✓ Determine whether any portion of your business shares in any variety of these traits.

✓ Consider your industry as a whole and make sure your marketing plan is competitive but unique enough to allow your business to stand out.

✓ If your current plan is not working as well as you'd like, there is a chance you've either strayed too far from the norm or you've been drowned out by your competition. Consider ways to improve your strategy by diverging from the norm or reeling in your abstract ideas.

Chapter 10

Business Theory

- Pricing
- Ethics
- Referrals
- New-Business Ideas
- Business Names
- Action Plan

Marketing and advertising are two of the most integral parts of any small business. They're not an electric bill that gets addressed five minutes out of every month. They're a comprehensive part of your company that is interwoven into almost all aspects of your business. It makes sense that something so crucial to your business also dictates the way you handle other parts of your operation. This chapter will talk about the links between varying aspects of your business and marketing strategy.

Pricing

Pricing is affected by a variety of conditions. Your costs must be covered, you'd like to make a profit, *and* you have to consider your competition's pricing. Are you offering a higher quality product or service for more money? Are you setting out to beat everyone else's price just to get business?

Advertising can play a major role in pricing, most of which is advantageous to you as a business owner. Your advertising sales reps may try to give you a similar version of my sentiments as they try to sell you a product, but I encourage you to look at these concepts objectively, as I am here as your marketing advocate.

Lowering Prices

Lowering your prices so that they compromise your profit margin is *not* a good marketing strategy!

In an attempt to secure more sales, businesses often lower their prices. They may be getting fewer calls, bids, or people through the door, so they lower prices in an attempt to encourage people to make buying decisions. This can have disastrous effects on your business. Compromising your profit margin or even eliminating it completely can cause obvious problems for your company.

I've been there before. Early in the painting season, when I get some of my first calls of the year, I have to fight the urge to compromise my pricing to improve my chances of having my bids accepted. Fortunately, I have always committed to a marketing plan that will allow me enough calls to charge a fair price, even at the risk of not converting sales.

Without an effective marketing program in place, there is no real way to know you're going to get enough calls to sustain your business. This can make you fear missing out on business so that in turn you price your product or service far too low. This can turn into a vicious cycle. You set your prices too low, and your costs and overhead start to catch up to you. All of a sudden, your future sales become even more important, so you stick to this lowered price or lower it more out of desperation.

I don't mean to sound as if I'm insulting people's business sense, but I'm not sure how so many people get the idea that if business is bad, lowering prices will bring in more people. Unless you have a marketing plan in place, no one will know about your lower prices. If you have a marketing plan in place, you probably won't need to resort to lower prices to save your business. As I stated earlier, some companies base their profits on lower prices, but that only works with a *higher volume*.

I know this sounds as if I'm setting up for a big rah-rah for advertising (which I am), but before you can even implement a better marketing strategy, there are things you can do.

Keep your prices in place and focus on improving your sales pitch. Some people are uncomfortable doing things that may seem pushy. If, as a hairstylist, you need to charge $30 per cut to comfortably stay in business, charge $30. When someone says, "Wow, $30!" don't immediately rethink your pricing. Instead, strengthen it by backing up your product: "Thirty dollars may seem like a lot, but we do X, Y, Z and use high-end products to give you the best haircut in town!" Wavering on your price devalues your product and service. Standing by and *selling* your product adds value.

Compromising on your price devalues your product; actively selling it adds value.

Continuing with the hairstylist example, if your average cost per session is $15, you're looking to make $30. If you drop your price just by $10, it will take you three times as long to make the profit you initially set out to make! Just take a look:

$30 − $15 cost = $15 profit

$20 − $15 cost = $5 profit

If you're worried about the number of people calling on your business, lowering your price and requiring *more* customers to make a profit simply will not work. You must stick to your initial pricing and create a marketing plan that works.

Raising Prices

One of the most common objections I came across when selling advertising was, "I already have more business than I can handle!" Sometimes it was just an excuse not to be solicited, but other times it was quite clear that it was the case. Because I was in the process of selling something to these business owners, the last thing I wanted to do was tell them how to run their business. Now that I'm not selling anyone anything, here is the message I've always wanted to convey....

If you have more business than you can handle, there are two things you can do (unless you are truly and utterly 100-percent satisfied with your business situation). First, you can expand. Take on more employees or more managers or expand your location— whatever you need to do to accommodate these extra sales. Remember the entrepreneurial attitude you had when you started your business and grow! Grow your business size and grow your profits.

If you have more business than you can handle, either grow your business or raise your prices.

Because there is some added risk with taking on more overhead, such as employees or space, consider option two....

Raise your prices. I've always wanted to tell this to business owners who thought they had it all figured out because they had more business than they could handle. This isn't a circumstance to brag about, because it says you lack some certain business savvy. This says to me that you've either left money on the table because you couldn't expand to meet your demands *or* you're not charging enough and you have weak margins. I'm sure you can see why I didn't want to use my natural objection when talking to these business owners....

Let's assume Larry's Lawn Service can only handle the maintenance on 100 lawns per month. Larry charges $50 per lawn and makes $25 profit, thus he profits $2,500 per month. Larry is also too busy to handle anymore work, so he turns down 20 referrals each month.

Let's say Larry and I have a long talk, and he increases his price per lawn to $60 per month. The price increase costs him 20 percent of his clients! Now he only has 80 customers.

Remember those 20 referrals he had to turn down? Twenty percent of them are no longer interested because of the increase, so there are only 16 additional people seeking his service. Larry now has 96 clients.

Now Larry's profits are $3,360 per month. He just gave himself a $10,320 annual raise with four fewer clients.

Larry also could have chosen to take on an employee to handle the extra potential business. What he loses in margins by adding the employee, he can make up for and profit in volume.

The point of this example is that your pricing should be maximized to the point where you are working at a comfortable capacity but not leaving too many people, if any at all, at the door.

Let's say Larry gets even bolder. "I'm the best guy in town. I'm going to charge $100 per lawn!"

Larry loses almost half of his clients. He's down to 50 clients—how sad. But profits are up to $3,750 for half the work!

Now we've taken the example beyond maximizing his income while working to a capacity. He's cut his workload and actually increased his profit by requiring more money for the quality of service he is providing.

Of course this is an easy-to-navigate and extreme example, but it should help you get past the "I have too much business to advertise" objection. Advertising gives you an abundance of customers from whom you can pick and choose. One of those choices you can make includes customers who are willing to pay more. Your advertising program may bring a thousand people to your door, but you have the right to charge more because you are choosing from a wider base of active customers. If you have a lower base of customers to choose from because you have not been advertising appropriately, you'll have less opportunity to get more for your services.

Conversion Rate

A very good way to test your pricing is by basing it on your conversion rate. If you turn every call into a paying customer, it's likely that you're not charging enough for your product or

Test your pricing by basing it on your conversion rate.

services. If you're only converting one out of a hundred, you're probably charging too much. Of course, this is all assuming you're offering real and competitive services. Different industries may expect to convert a different percentage of customers, but it's still a great way to gauge your pricing. You charged $50 for a normal pizza, got 100 calls, and only sold one; obviously, you need to lower your price. If a roofer only charges $2,000 to replace a roof (and he's legitimately going to do the work in a decent fashion), his 100-percent conversion rate may prove that his pricing is way too low.

This can be tied into marketing, because a greater number of calls can give you more wiggle room to adjust your conversion rate. If an accountant is only getting four calls per month, she'd better convert three, if not all of them. If she's getting 20 calls per month, she can price better for her bottom line, only convert 25 percent, but still get five customers paying the price that she wants for a higher profit margin.

Ethics

With the growing number of scams and the amount of fraud going on in the United States, people are becoming more and more leery about who they choose to do business with on a daily basis. This is why positive referrals are important to any business. People like to hear about the quality of your product or service through a reliable source before they conduct business with you.

False Advertising

False advertising isn't always an obvious infraction. A sub shop that runs an ad for a $4 sub but actually charges people $8 for that sub is using false advertising in the most blatant sense. A pure lie about a price, product, or service to get people in the door is false advertising.

Fees, additional costs, and required up-selling tend to be the most common ways a business can get in trouble for false advertising. When a limo service offers a car and driver for $199 for three hours in an advertisement, people expect to pay $199 plus tax (and for most people with common courtesy, a tip). If at the end of the service, you find out about a $35 gas fee and a $45 maintenance charge, and the company made no mention of these added costs in their commercial or anywhere in their sales pitch, the limo service is guilty of false advertising.

This is why whenever you see a price that looks too good to be true, you're almost certain to find some "fine print." These are little notices that denote extra fees and charges that may be associated with the final cost of your transaction. This helps companies legally cover themselves for charging more than the big, bold price splashed across the pages.

For business owners, this practice can be a tossup. I personally suggest going with the industry standard so that people do not end up feeling misled. Everyone buying a cell phone knows that $39.99 is not going to be the final cost. You advertise the price, you include your fine print, and most of the time things work out smoothly. If a florist, on the other hand, offered a Mother's Day bouquet for $39.99 but charged a bunch of fees, people would not respond quite as well, even if there was fine print included.

Besides pricing, you can also be accused of false advertising if you claim to offer a certain product or service to get someone in the door, but then you have no real way of making that offer come to fruition. Of course there will be occasions when product runs out or something makes it impossible for the offer to be upheld. This is why it's crucial to either note "while supplies last" in your marketing materials *or* offer a rain check, the way most grocery stores do. If you do none of these things and habitually are out of these products or services, you may get a letter from your state's attorney general.

Forced up-selling is one of the most malicious forms of false advertising. Yes, fees and extra charges can be a hassle, but forcing extra purchases will have people spreading the word about your ethically challenged business. Let's say a spa dealer offers a six-person hot tub for $3,999 through an online banner ad. A consumer clicks through and sees the website with the same offer and pictures of people enjoying a hot tub, with the price plastered everywhere on the site. Nowhere on the site does it say anything about added charges or fees, so the consumer heads into the store. When he arrives, the salesperson shows him the $3,999 spa. The customer agrees to make the purchase, and he and the salesperson go to the counter to complete the transaction. The salesperson begins writing up an invoice. "Let's see, $3,999 for the spa, $859 for the motor, $485 for the pump...." The customer tells the salesperson he just wants the basic $3,999 hot tub, but he is informed that it requires the other things to function correctly.

This company depicted a spa for sale at a fixed price and added on items that were required to make it work. Many things could happen to this business. First, the customer might cave and just foot the entire bill. Second, the customer could give the salesperson a piece of his mind and spend a considerable amount of time badmouthing the company. And finally, the customer could (and should) report the store to the state attorney general's office.

If someone is reported to the state attorney general's office for false advertising or any other business infraction, the attorney general's office usually reviews the circumstances on a case-by-case basis. Every business doing any kind of real volume can expect someone to get upset about something and turn to the attorney general. However, if the attorney general's office starts to pile up complaints, they will force you to take action or face charges.

Discounts

Be sure your discounts come off your *normal* price, not an inflated price.

Ethically speaking, discounts should be discounts from a normal price. If a photographer offers a coupon for $200 off any wedding, it should be $200 off the established base price. Some businesses will add on the $200 before making the deduction, making the discount just a bunch of smoke and mirrors. This, too, can fall under the umbrella of false advertising, but you're more likely to build a bad reputation. This kind of dishonesty is hard for people with fixed and published prices to pull off, so it is seen more with people giving fresh price quotes.

Whenever I see a coupon that says, "Must present before price is quoted," it's an immediate red flag that the person will be adding on before subtracting. Not all consumers know this. I know this, and you know this now too, so consider sticking to "may not be combined with any other discounts." That way, if you work out a discount for your customers, and then they throw their coupons out at the last second, you do not have to reach deeper into your pockets.

The way to avoid destroying your margin or having coupons hurt you is simply to have high enough prices that you have wiggle room to cut your prices. If consumers are comparing quotes and all things are equal, they will likely take the quote that included a coupon. For example, let's assume someone is getting a quote on repairing his transmission, and he goes to two different mechanics. The first mechanic quotes $1,200. The second mechanic quotes $1,400, but the customer has a $200 off transmission services coupon. The reality is that both mechanics would be charging $1,200. However, assuming the customer is completely split down the line on the quality and his knowledge of the shops, he will almost certainly go with the mechanic offering the discount.

Referrals

Referrals are the best way to get business. Marketing and advertising grows your referral base and business exponentially. Treating your customers right and giving them what they expect or better will keep them coming back and giving you referrals.

If your business is based on low prices and higher volume, people are willing to give up some level of quality, knowing they're getting a better price. However, this does not mean that they will be okay with junk or a service that fails. Keep people's expectations real, and they will appreciate your low prices for what they are. If you try to say you have the best quality and the lowest prices, you'll likely come up short on one of the two, and you'll kill your chances of referral and repeat business.

If your business is based on reasonable or even higher rates but also higher quality, you *must* provide a product or service better than that of most of your competition. In most cases, you cannot get away with simply charging more without providing a better experience.

Most of these concepts may seem to go without saying, but it's important to understand that standing by these theories will ensure you a solid referral base.

Let's follow this spectrum of service to better understand how referrals will work.

1. Andy charges $40 for an hour-long massage. The place is a dump and smells bad. Andy barely moves his hands and is talking on his cell phone the whole time. The customer consensus? "Andy was a complete waste of time. The price was low, but it was a disgusting place and a waste of time. Avoid him at all costs!" Andy will never get a referral.

2. Betty charges $40 for an hour-long massage. The sheets are clean, there is soft music playing, and the room smells fresh. Betty does a pretty basic massage, but she uses the right amount of pressure. There's a noisy office next door but nothing too distracting. The customer consensus? "Betty's treatment area was nice and basic, she gave an attentive massage, and it was well worth it at 40 bucks." Betty will get referrals and will certainly see her clients on a regular basis.

3. Carrie charges $40 for an hour-long massage. There is a waiting room with several free drink options. The table is heated, and Carrie uses the finest cotton sheets money can buy. She uses a wide range of aromatherapy products and has a vast knowledge of techniques. Her massages frequently run 20 minutes over. The customer consensus? "Carrie gave the most incredible massage, and it was only $40! You *must* go see her, because there's no way she's going to stay in business for long at that price." The customer said it best; from earlier, you'll remember that Carrie is leaving too much money on the table. Her margin is already small because of the extra products she's offering. She will burn out and/or go out of business quickly if she doesn't adjust her prices.

4. Denise charges $180 for an hour-long massage. Her practice is similar to Carrie's. She also has a sauna and a steam room for clients to use before and after their treatments. Her technique is second to none. The customer consensus? "Denise charged a lot for her massage, but it's one I'll never forget! I will certainly come back again for a special occasion. You guys should go see her next month for your anniversary!" Denise will get referrals as well. She may not get the frequency of visits that Betty does, but people book her up well in advance for special occasions or just an extravagant treat. She also has clearly built in enough profit margin to remain in business for as long as she chooses.

5. Edward charges $180 for an hour-long massage. His massage table is in an average office. The room is cold, and his massage is rough but efficient. He's watching the clock the whole time. The customer consensus? "I don't know how Edward thinks he can charge $180 for a massage! His office was unappealing, and the massage was definitely subpar." Edward will not get any referrals. People may be fooled once to spend more money than something's worth, but when they realize your product or service doesn't deliver, you'll never see them again.

Two people had great success with their business plan—Betty and Denise. Betty has reasonable rates and passable service. Denise charges far more, but she's providing more. She may not see her clients as often, but her profit margin makes that okay. These two would benefit greatly from different advertising plans. Betty can splash her prices where she wants, while Denise must focus on her quality and the overall experience.

Andy used low prices to get people in the door, but his service wasn't even passable. He won't get referrals or repeat business. Advertising may bring in some people, but there's no way he'll be able to afford an effective marketing program for long enough to burn through every consumer.

Carrie did a great job and will get referrals, but she won't be able to sustain the quality on such a low profit margin. The small marketing program she can afford may bring in some people, but she'll be working for peanuts.

Edward charged as if he was high end, but he provided a second-rate experience. People will not return to him because there is no perceived value in his services. A strong advertising campaign would likely keep him in business longer than Andy and Carrie because of his profit margin, but there are only so many bridges you can burn in a town before the word gets out that your service isn't worth it.

Betty and Denise were the real winners of this exercise, but let's tie this all back into marketing. What if Betty tried to market herself as having the lowest prices in town but the *best* service around and the most beautiful workspace? People would still come in. Most would be happy about the price, but the lower quality would leave them feeling misled. Consumers don't always know that lower prices and high quality cannot really go together. Betty should feature the price as her marketing focal point and simply convey that she offers a professional massage in a clean and comfortable environment.

Denise is the high-end provider, but let's assume she had a similar advertising program. "Best service and best prices in town!" She may get people in the door, but a large majority would turn around and walk back out. Her services may be the best, but many people would never know because her prices certainly aren't the lowest.

As you can see, marketing and advertising are two of the most important parts of anyone's small business. They're intermingled with many more facets of business than most people know. Making sure you have a healthy marketing strategy will ensure that the other aspects of your business will succeed.

New-Business Ideas

To start a new business, take someone else's business idea and do it better.

Many people assume that starting a new business means coming up with a brand-new business idea or industry. "How about a place where you can eat tacos *and* get your hair washed at the same time?! No one has ever done *that* before!" There is always room for innovation in a free market society, but there has to be a sensible demand for your product or service. Just because no one has done it, that doesn't mean someone wants you to! But if you truly are on the cutting edge of technology or have the opportunity to ride the wave of a new fad or trend, there certainly is room for brand-new business ideas.

My father always told me that starting a new business is about taking someone else's business idea and doing it better. There may be dozens of companies replacing windows in your town, but there's nothing stopping you from starting your own window-replacement company. Go ahead and compete, but make sure you have something better to offer so you can compete with and win over the other companies in town. Maybe you have a faster turnaround time or higher quality or even lower prices, for example. No matter what part of the business model you plan to improve on, make sure it includes an effective marketing strategy.

Business Names

If you haven't already named or branded your business, there are certain things you should consider before setting a name in stone. But before you read this section, simply read through these names:

- B&R
- CCM
- J.R.
- F&N
- SLS
- Lampson's Luxury Autos
- N.E.C. Co.
- W.R. Inc.

We'll come back to these in a bit....

A Names

One of the oldest tricks in the book (no pun intended) is to start your business with an A name so you will appear first in alphabetical lists—namely, the Yellow Pages. Although this may give you a slight advantage when people are calling straight down the listings, it will hurt you in most of your other marketing moves. First, keep in mind that people who call off of the listings as opposed to ads in the phone book generally call as many people as they can. That being said, you'd better have some low prices and be immediately available when they call, or your potential client will move right on to the Bs. Second, these kinds of "AAA,"

"Able," or "American" names are virtually unbrandable in the sea of other business owners who had the same idea. If you *must* compete alphabetically, at least use a unique A word or name that will sound memorable and respectable in your other advertising mediums.

Abbreviations

Abbreviated business names are a form of branding suicide. Abbreviations rarely stick in people's memories, and they take far longer to brand than a unique name. Remember Lampson's Luxury Autos from earlier in this section? Remember any of the others? If you saw an ad in the paper for Lampson's Luxury Autos right next to one for SLS, you'd likely remember the first of the two businesses for a much longer time, and you'd be able to pick out their name quickly in future publications. Even if the abbreviation is followed by an industry, it still won't work as well as a full and memorable word or name. C.D. Paving is far less memorable than Curtis Devin Paving, for example.

Common Names

No offense, Mr. Smith, but we're going to have to find your company a better name! Be honest with yourself: A common last name is not going to brand as well as a unique one. Although throwing your name into your business certainly makes your ego feel good, it won't have the marketing appeal of a more unique moniker.

In addition to common names, avoid played-out words that pop, such as Best, Superior, Prime, #1, Discount, and other such words that you've seen thousands of times in your travels.

Action Plan

As the final part of your action plan, ask yourself these questions:

✓ How does your pricing compare to the rest of your industry?

✓ How can you work on your sales pitch to qualify the value of your pricing?

✓ Are you leaving any money on the table?

✓ What's the *highest* price you could charge without hurting your business?

✓ Are you running your business ethically?

✓ How strong is your referral base?

✓ Are you painting an honest picture of yourself to consumers so that they know what to expect from your product or service?

✓ If your business is in a brand-new industry, is there a real market for your product or service?

✓ Is it too late to change your business name if it falls into one of the less effective categories?

Chapter 11

New Businesses

- Insufficient Capital
- Bad Location
- No Market
- Overexpansion
- Fierce Competition
- Poor Customer Service
- Building a New Business Marketing Plan
- The No-Money Startup
- Free Advertising
- Action Plan

Most new businesses fail within the first four years of their existence. There are a variety of explanations and excuses for these short-lived ventures. I'm here to tell you that the main—and virtually only—reason new businesses fail is a poor marketing strategy. Proper marketing should bring in enough revenue to knock out most of the problems or at least give you some wiggle room until they are solved.

This chapter will present some of the top problems that experts say shut the doors of many new businesses and how they can be mitigated by proper marketing.

Insufficient Capital

What is the one way you can combat insufficient capital? By bringing in more money! If you start your business with limited funds, and sales are trickling in on a limited basis, there is no way you'll have enough money to stay afloat. So how do you increase sales? With better marketing. When you're starting a new business, most of your limited resources need to be directed at marketing your business.

Bad Location

A great location will only yield excellent returns if you have a marketing budget and strategy to maximize your customer base.

The old saying, "location, location, location," in reality can only take you so far. As you likely already know, prime locations come with a hefty price tag. Suppose you want to open an insurance agency on the busiest corner of your city, and rent will run you $10,000 per month. You'd likely get more unsolicited walk-ins than any of your competitors, and the high traffic would lead to some branding (assuming you have proper signage).

Two miles away, there's a commercial park that's renting the same size space for $2,000 per month. Now you've got far less pedestrian and auto traffic, but you have an extra $8,000 in your pocket each month. I'm sure you can see where I'm going with this. I'll even venture to say that the business in a less exposed area with an $8,000 monthly marketing budget likely will do far better than the business in a prime spot with no money left to advertise.

Just remember, the old adage comes true if you're in a bad location *and* you have no marketing strategy. With the proper mix of advertising, your customers will be coming to you, no matter what your location. If you do end up in a high-traffic area, just make sure you have more than enough signage to capitalize on all the free traffic.

No Market

Says who? Unless your business idea is so farfetched that no one needs your product or service, there is always a way to find and solicit your market. The only catch is that the market may not be right outside your door. If you have a product or service that isn't limited to geographical area, proper advertising on the Internet can help you target your primary market regardless of where they may be.

There's always a way to find and solicit your market.

If your business requires face-to-face contact, such as a restaurant business, things become a little trickier. A Kenyan restaurant could certainly thrive in the U.S., but you may not have a lot of luck in a smaller town with no African influence or one primarily made up of people who are used to very specific foods. This is an example of a business where the market exists—you just have to physically transplant there.

Sometimes "no market" is confused with "small market." If you own a home-improvement company that installs indoor swimming pools, you'll have a smaller market that takes very well-targeted advertising. You could blow your money on television advertising to half a million people when only a few hundred would even consider your service—*or* you could direct-mail based on income levels. Tweaking your marketing strategy to seek out those smaller markets will keep you from thinking there is *no* market.

Overexpansion

Overexpansion is obviously a problem if you do not have the sales to back up the increasing overhead. This is really a sub-problem to insufficient capital. If you blow your money on expanding for the sake of expanding, of course your business is going to fail. If you grow your business on pace with the increased sales you've generated through marketing, expansion is a good thing!

Grow your business on pace with your increasing sales. Do not expand just to expand!

You must always be careful before you expand your business. It might be great to hire more employees or get another store-front with your added income, but what if you reinvested that income into even more advertising for your business? Unless you've reached your working capacity, bring in more business before you set out to expand.

Fierce Competition

Have you ever heard of Burger King or Wendy's? Of course you have. They compete with one of the largest companies in the world, yet they are still successful businesses in their own right. How do they stay competitive? Marketing.

When in a fiercely competitive market, it's doubly important to have a strong marketing strategy.

The same holds true on the local- and small-business level. The number-one heating and air conditioning company in town may have a full-page ad in the Yellow Pages and a full-page ad in each month's coupon magazine. What's to say you can't go out and do the same thing? Take out full-page ads and make better offers! Of course the number-one company will have the advantage of reputation working for them, but if you get out there and compete head to head, you will certainly get a piece of the pie.

Where you will come up short is if you come out against fierce competition with no real marketing strategy. If you're a personal-injury lawyer, and you only committed to a little banner ad somewhere online and a bold listing in the Yellow Pages, you might as well send your resume to the firms you see all over the television all day long.

Poor Customer Service

Poor customer service results when you have a problem running the day-to-day aspects of your business: Your product or service is poor, and people don't want to do business with you. Although I would never suggest doing this, there are plenty of companies out there who get two thumbs down from the consumer but stay in business simply because they keep marketing. Effective marketing *could* allow you to churn and burn customers, but I suggest that you improve your business practices instead. An advertisement with poor service is only worth one customer at a time, but with proper customer service, referrals will come streaming in. Use your marketing to bring in more sales to keep your business afloat, but be sure to address your customer-service issues to be successful in the long run.

Building a New Business Marketing Plan

Using the information you've learned in this book will help you build an effective marketing strategy at a reasonable investment. When it comes to new business, you can use those same techniques, but here are a few additional things to consider when your business venture is just taking off. This is the most crucial, make-or-break time for your business, and marketing *must* be your number-one priority.

Start Early

Many people make the mistake of opening a business and then focusing on marketing after it's up and running. This mistake will cause you to eat up much of your capital before you can start reaping the benefits of your advertisements. Remember, building a marketing strategy is not just about picking up the phone and ordering an ad; it's about educating yourself and learning about your local market. Also, some mediums can take a very long time from initial contact to your advertising being public. Phonebooks operate on a yearly basis, magazines are filled months in advance, commercials take time to produce, and even building print-ad copy can be time consuming.

Before you open your doors, order a phone line, or even leave your prior position to start your own business, start meeting with sales reps. You do not have to qualify your business to them; all they want to do is sell you on their medium. You don't even need your business certificate! Let them know you're going into business soon, but you want your advertising in place so that you can hit the ground running.

Have your advertising already in place when you open your new business's doors.

This process will allow you to learn all about the different types of advertising in your community without the stresses of running a business with no clients on a day-to-day basis. Also, this will give you an opportunity to compute your initial startup costs. Some advertising companies will require money or a portion of your bill upfront. Remember that even some of these terms are negotiable. Meeting with as many salespeople as possible will allow you to know who's offering what terms and how to get the most effective advertising at reasonable costs and for as little upfront money as possible. Later on in your self-employment life, you can look upon advertising costs as more of an investment, but early on the money has to come from your startup funds.

Start Big

If you want to hit the ground running with sales coming in as soon as you open your doors, you must start off with a substantial advertising program. If anything, marketing dollars should eat up the largest part of your budget early on. Get as many coupons and offers in the hands of consumers as is financially possible. You want to generate sales quickly so that you can eliminate any kind of building-up time or stress on your dwindling startup egg.

Remember from earlier examples in this book that call-to-action ads are the best way to generate quick sales. Get people in the doors before you start branding your business. When people are comfortable with your product or service, you can spend some of the bigger dollars on branding-style marketing.

Grand Opening

Use the novelty and freshness of your new business as a way to drive your initial sales. Offer discounts and advertise them as a way to get people hooked on your product or service. You can still build profit into these sales as long as your margin is big enough. As long as consumers feel as if you're giving deep discounts to get them in the door, this strategy will work.

Along with hanging the usual grand-opening banners, offer incentives to get customers in the door during your grand-opening day, week, or month.

Grand-opening signs are not the way to have a grand opening. My heart sinks when I drive by a business with grand-opening banners and an empty storefront. The signs are fine, but make sure they're backed up with proper marketing and offers to drive people to your business in a timely fashion. Put out coupons that are only good for your grand-opening day, week, or month. Use radio or television to announce your new business, but still include huge offers to get people to attend your grand-opening event.

This may sound appropriate only for retail and storefront businesses, but it can hold true for any industry. Professionals can offer free consultations and discounts or even throw open-house events or mixers. Service businesses can offer deep discounts celebrating their opening and give away free gifts or upgrades to their first customers. Any creative and bold offer or event can help kick off a business if it is properly marketed. However, these businesses may be more suited for the following option.

"Secret" Opening

This is one of the most unorthodox methods of starting a new business, but it can be one of the most effective ways to drive initial sales. For a variety of reasons, consumers can be scared off by new businesses. If you think that may be true for your industry, consider this strategy.

Advertise as if you've been in business for years. Now, before you think I'm suggesting that you lie in your advertising, hear me out. I'm not telling you to say, "since 1967" or "thousands of satisfied customers." If you do that, your state's attorney general will find you and shut you down. I'm saying that you can skip over any kind of grand opening or announcement of your business being new.

Consider hiding the fact that you're a brand-new business by emphasizing your strengths and offerings rather than broadcasting a grand opening.

There are plenty of businesses in your town that have been around for decades and that some people have never heard of. A homeowner may never consider who the roofers in town are until it's time to replace his roof. But when he needs a new roof, he'll start noticing roofers' ads or even search for one online or in the phone book. If he comes across your ad in a magazine, and the ad just talks about your quality materials and procedures and that you have some good offers, the homeowner will likely give you a call. In the magazine you might be right next to another roofer that has been in business since 1955, but you still have a fair shot at getting calls. If your ad makes a big deal about a grand opening, the homeowner may question your experience or professionalism.

Chances are you're opening a business in which you have some kind of experience. Although you can't legally say you've been in business since 1999, there's nothing wrong with saying that you have 12 years of experience. Maybe you've decided to open your own auto-repair shop because your father and grandfather did the same thing. Why not advertise that you're a third-generation auto mechanic? The only thing that separates a new business from an old one is years in business and number of customers served. Feel free to avoid addressing either of those points and instead focus on the strengths of your company.

Either of these two openings can help your business start off on the right foot as long as you keep your finances focused heavily on marketing. Remember, just cutting checks to different advertising companies isn't going to cause the dollars to come rolling in. Follow the advice from earlier chapters and make educated marketing investments.

The No-Money Startup

You won't necessarily have buckets of money at your disposal to start a business. Some people decide to become entrepreneurs because they are currently unemployed or because money is the problem to begin with.

I'm not here to give you some magical solution that is guaranteed to work with no money down. But I will say that unless it is your absolute last-ditch effort at taking care of yourself and your family, under no circumstances should you start a business with no upfront capital. That being said, let's investigate what your options are if you don't have any startup money.

First, retail and restaurant businesses are out of the question. You cannot get a storefront without parting with some money. This leaves you with service-type businesses and anything you can do out of your home. Still, marketing these businesses can be tricky.

As with any new company, you must meet with as many advertising salespeople as possible. The only difference now is that you are trying to find a company that will let you commence advertising either on credit or with no money down. I understand that this is a huge roll of the dice, but I'm assuming you're doing this because you are backed into a corner in the first place.

I'm sure some people with money to spend on a startup are wondering why they can't do the same thing when starting *their* business. The answer is quite simple. If you limit yourself to advertising only with companies that do not want money upfront, you'll be missing out on most of the real opportunity in your market. Searching for advertising with no money down is only advisable in a worst-case scenario.

No-money-down advertising is only a smart plan if you have absolutely *no* startup money to use for advertising.

When you've found a few mediums you can work with, you must build a program without considering your financial circumstances. If you worry about being able to pay the bills, you'll under-buy out of fear, get little to no response, and ruin your credit when you can't pay these newfound bills.

As you learned earlier in this book when we talked about pricing, the biggest mistake you can make now is compromising your pricing. It's understandable that you may feel desperate in these early stages of your business, but if you allow your profit margin to shrink, your business will not survive. You must still make great offers to bring in potential clients, but make sure that even after discounts you still have a large enough profit margin built into your pricing.

In these tight circumstances, in addition to finding advertising for no money down, try to keep your focus on print and online ads. You will not survive long enough to meet the Yellow Pages cycle, and without a number there, radio and television will not be very effective. Stick to mediums where people will have your number right in front of them when they are ready to call your business.

After what will likely be one of the most stressful months of your life, you should be able to bring in enough business to operate on a normal new-business cycle. This doesn't mean you should go out and start buying all kinds of equipment and a new storefront, though. Keep your focus on marketing until you have enough money to sustain your campaign and *then* grow your business.

Free Advertising

There are some places online where you can list your business information for free, and you can always put up flyers for almost no cost. You can use these venues in conjunction with more affordable startup options, but relying solely on these mediums simply will not work. If these were highly profitable resources for businesses to advertise through, they would not be free.

Action Plan

If you're a new business owner, it is important for you to answer these questions before you go out on your own. If you don't address your marketing needs early enough, you'll end up running out of time and money.

✓ What are some potential ways your new business could fail?

✓ How can you address these issues through your marketing plan?

✓ What kind of opening would work best for your business?

✓ What features and benefits can you focus on in lieu of years in business and customers served?

✓ What is the maximum amount of money you can put toward an advertising program?

Remember to review the earlier chapters and build a marketing strategy *before* you build your business!

Index